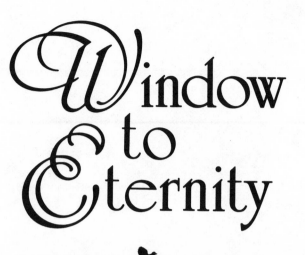

Window to Eternity

Bruce Henderson

The Swedenborg Foundation
New York

WINDOW TO ETERNITY
First Printing 1987

ISBN 0-87785-132-8
Library of Congress Catalog Card Number 86-6038

Cover design by Nancy Crompton
Book design by John N. Tierney
Copyediting by Suzanne C. Gagne

Manufactured in the United States of America

Swedenborg Foundation, Inc.
139 East 23rd Street
New York, New York 10010

To my Father
who helped so many
to understand

Guide to Footnote Abbreviations

Books by Emanuel Swedenborg:
AC—Arcana Coelestia
AE—Apocalypse Explained
CL—Conjugial Love
HH—Heaven and Hell
SD—Spiritual Diary

Bible quotations are taken from the King James version of The Sacred Scripture.
(See Bibliograpy for all publication details.)

Contents

Introduction

A little girl asks, "Daddy, what happens when you die?" It is one of those questions daddies struggle to answer. And all her life she wonders: Is death the end of life? Is it like going to sleep, only I never wake up? Or does something inside of me begin a new life, without this body? What kind of a life could that be? Am I still going to be a real person, or some kind of a ghost?

What about Granny and Grandfather? Are they still alive somewhere? Will I ever see them again? Will they still be old? Will they still know me?

Is there really a "book of life"? Is someone going to read it and decide if I should go to heaven or to hell?

What about angels? Do they really have wings and harps and halos? Do devils have horns? Do they live in fire? Is heaven really as great as they say? And no matter how great, doesn't it get a little boring . . . ?

The questions never go away. Sometimes they go profoundly deeper. Sometimes they never lose that childlike wonder. For the answers often seem so hard to find. But the mystery of death no longer needs to be bewildering.

We have been getting glimpses of what happens after death from people who have died, been resuscitated, and come back to life after strikingly consistent out-of-body experiences. Popular books such as *On Death and Dying* by Dr. Elizabeth Kübler-Ross and *Life After Life* by Dr. Raymond A. Moody, Jr., have helped to bring death out of the closets of the mind. People are willing to think about death, and the more they understand it, the less they are afraid.

This new attitude about death has spread far beyond hospitals and research clinics. Death has become a vital part of many high school and college curriculums. Books expound new theories and experiences. The media have discovered that death is something more than a headline.

Those who have lived to tell about the "death experience" have helped rekindle faith in a life after death. Dr. Kübler-Ross concedes that the evidence does not prove anything, but that "there are common denominators you can't deny."

Those who have returned from the death experience don't fear death anymore. They "know" that they will live in a better world because they are convinced they have seen it. But while they have helped to open the minds of skeptics, there are many questions they have not answered.

More than two hundred years ago, however, a complete description of the life after death was written by Emanuel Swedenborg, one of the foremost scientists, philosophers, theologians, and intellects of his or any time. This insight was part of what he humbly asserted was a whole new revelation from God. It lays out the internal or hidden meanings of the Bible and its parables and clarifies, for many of us, the spiritual significance of our lives.

Swedenborg wrote more than thirty volumes of closely reasoned doctrine during the last twenty-seven years of an amazingly productive life. Included within them is the description—still unknown through much of the world, but full of lucid detail—of the spiritual life that awaits us.

If this description is as complete and accurate as Swedenborg claims it is fair to ask, Why isn't it better known?

The writings of Swedenborg are accepted by people all over the world as the basis for a "new Christianity." But their numbers are relatively small. People must have doubts and questions before they will be receptive to anything new. Now the acceptance of openly questioning death has led many to search deeper for answers and to discover Swedenborg.

In his book *Life After Life*, Dr. Raymond A. Moody cites four "striking parallels" to what he learned in studying the experience of dying: the Bible, the writings of Plato, the Tibetan Book of the Dead, and the writings of Emanuel Swedenborg. Of these, the writings of Swedenborg offer the most extensive description of the life after death available to us.[1]

What Swedenborg writes about heaven and hell is fascinating, in implication and detail. His account doesn't prove anything about life after death, either. Absolute proof would take away our freedom to believe what we choose to believe. It would virtually compel faith. But the wealth of detail and the reasonable way it is presented testify that this is not just one man's fanciful imagination; it is a special vision.

Swedenborg's insight can make a big difference in your life. It can help to make you more confident and less fearful about the life after death by taking away much of the anxiety and the unknowns about death and showing it as part of a natural progression of life, not its end.

You may give little thought in this busy world to an everlasting life after death, and even less to the likelihood that it will be determined by the way you live your life here. But Swedenborg makes clear that the conscious and unconscious choices that shape your character also shape your destiny.

Swedenborg emphasizes that it is not specific choices or actions that determine whether you will go to heaven or to hell. It is the pattern of all your choices and the motivation behind them that make heaven or hell the only home for your spirit. That includes everything in your life—from how you react to small things, such as being cut off in traffic, to major life decisions.

So the ultimate question in life becomes, Am I choosing, by the way I live my life, an eternity of happiness in heaven or a never-ending life of frustration and ugliness in hell? Swedenborg warns that you are making that choice all through your life. That does not mean that you con-

1. Dr. Raymond A. Moody, *Life After Life* (Atlanta: Mockingbird Books, 1975), pp. 79-89.

stantly swing from one extreme to another, but that from the middle ground of your life you incline more and more to one or the other.

By now you may be asking yourself, Who is Emanuel Swedenborg that he claims to have special insight? Plenty of others have claimed revelation from God, and attracted more skeptics than believers. Swedenborg has his share of both, but most people who have read him are convinced that he was an extraordinary man and that his insight *is* something special. You have to decide for yourself whether it is divine revelation or just the product of one man's imagination. Bear in mind that as with Moses, revelation is one way that God has taught us. And it is one way that He can teach us about the life after death.

This book may change your thinking about death and change your life as well. It should help you to realize that even though death is difficult to accept, a deeper understanding of it can inspire comfort and confidence in the fact that death is really something greater: it is rebirth into life forever after.

The more you believe in an afterlife, the more it can influence your life in positive ways. And that faith can become a positive influence for others. The gentle loving sphere of a spiritual direction in life makes anyone a better person, and helps to make this a better world.

What does life mean? What does death mean? And what will it be like to die? These are troublesome questions for any parent. The spectrum of religious faiths in this world presents a confusion of claims and teachings. Swedenborg's writings lent his first-hand insight. The amazingly consistent death-experience reports open a door. They hint that death really is the beginning of a new life, and that it can be a much better life. They may help us to be less afraid. They may help us cope with the death we all must face. In Dr. Moody's reports, one experiencer said it "opened up a whole new world to me that I never knew could possibly exist."[2] Another said confidently that, "Now, I am not afraid to die. . . . I know where I'm going when I leave here, because I've been there before."[3]

But without the insight given through Swedenborg, these reports still do not give enough detail. Swedenborg describes not only his revelation of what death will be like, but what will follow. You can find new meaning in death—and life. Death, the one enduring mystery of life, is not so much a mystery anymore.

2. Ibid., p. 65.
3. Ibid., p. 69.

1

Mystery No More

Behold, I show you a mystery;
We shall not all sleep, but shall
all be changed.
—1 Corinthians 15:51

Today's churchman knows almost nothing about heaven, hell, or his own life after death, even though this is all described in the Word. It has gone so far that even many people born in the church deny these things and ask in their hearts, "Has anyone come back and told us?"

"To prevent so negative an attitude (which is particularly prevalent among people with much worldly wisdom) from infecting and corrupting people of simple heart and simple faith, it has been made possible for me to be as one with angels and to talk with them person to person. I have also been allowed to see what heaven is like and then what hell is like; this has been going on for thirteen years. So now I may describe heaven and hell from what I have seen and heard, hoping for the enlightenment of ignorance and the dispersion of disbelief by this means."[1]

So begins Emanuel Swedenborg's *Heaven and Hell*, a guidebook to the life after death from someone who was allowed to visit both. It provides a unique insight into the eternal life that awaits us.

We can add to Dante's *Inferno* and Milton's *Paradise Lost* another, more detailed, vision of the world of our spirit. We can escape Hamlet's symbolic "dread of something after death"[2] and not be afraid anymore. We can increase our understanding of life and death.

We see the cycles of life, death, and rebirth all the time. Spring flowers rise from winter's grave. A brilliant butterfly emerges from the caterpillar's tomb. But the idea of our soul or spirit surviving death is beyond our sight and experience. We long for assurance.

The Bible is filled with teachings about life after death, but not much detail. Swedenborg, under God's direction, adds detail. The heaven he describes is not a world of leisure, filled with harps and clouds and flitting wings. It is an incredibly beautiful place, similar to this world but with nothing of its ugliness and menace. True happiness is found there, not in idle luxury but in useful, active lives of kindness.

1. *HH*, Author's Preface, p. 12.
2. William Shakespeare, *Hamlet*, act 3, sc. 1.

We all know the joy of being caught up in doing things for people we love. The inhabitants of heaven feel that joy all the time. They are never selfish, always sharing. They would not be happy with a life of lazy self-indulgence. But heaven is not just being busy, either. There is plenty of recreation and social life. And there is never a hint of boredom.

Hell is just the opposite. Swedenborg found no friendship there because no one trusted anyone else. They lived for themselves, not the happiness of others. Instead of heaven's peace and happiness there was selfishness, deceit, ugliness, meanness, and frustration.

There is both warning and promise in this revelation about heaven and hell. The warning is that you are choosing one or the other right now, every day, by the way you choose to live your life. The promise is that you *can* dwell in a heavenly realm if that is where you really want to be.

The notion that heaven is the reward for a good life and hell the punishment for an evil life is simplistic. Swedenborg illustrates that it is not so much what you do in your life that determines whether you choose heaven or hell, but why you do it. It is the why—the reason you act as you do—that defines who you are. It is in forming that character, through a lifetime of free choices, that you choose life in heaven or hell. Whichever you choose becomes the fulfillment of the life you really want to live.

Swedenborg warns that after death it is too late to change who you are. But there is the promise, echoed in the Bible, that if you "do justly, and love mercy, and walk humbly with thy God,"[3] heaven is not hard to attain, because it becomes part of your life.

The peace and happiness we associate with heaven often seem elusive on earth because justice, mercy, and humility are just as rare. We live between our best aspirations and worst instincts, with both turmoil and tranquility in our lives and in the world around us. We are left to dream that somewhere there must be perfect justice and something better than this troubled world. But instead of calm assurance and resolute faith, people flounder over the meaning of life and its consequences.

Swedenborg found that angels in heaven were amazed at the ignorance on earth about the life after death. And they rejoiced when he told them that God was making that life known through this new revelation.

Talking to people who had just died and come into their spiritual life, he found them thrilled and surprised to be alive. They could hardly believe that they still looked the same—even that they had the same kind of clothes and houses—and had all the same feelings that made them the individuals they were.

"At the same time," Swedenborg writes, "they were amazed that they

3. Micah 6:8.

had been in such ignorance, such blindness about the condition of their own life after death. They were even more amazed that church folk were in the same kind of ignorance and blindness, when of all people in all lands of the earth, they could be in light in these matters."[4]

When Swedenborg asked them to recall what they had thought about the life after death while on this earth, "they are struck with shame and admit that they had thought nonsense, and that people of simple faith had thought far more wisely than they."[5]

He was acutely aware, however, of the problem of trying to make the spiritual world as real in our eyes as he saw it to be. He tells of angels asking him to assure friends on earth that they were very much alive and happy, "but I replied that were I to tell their friends such things, they would not believe; and I should merely expose myself to derision. That these things are true, perchance but few will believe."[6]

At the end of *Heaven and Hell* he says simply:

> What we have presented in this book about heaven, the world of spirits, and hell, will be obscure to people who find no delight in knowing spiritual truths; but they will be clear to people who do find this delight. This is particularly true for people involved in an affection for what is true for its own sake—that is, for people who love what is true because it is true. In fact, anything that is loved brings light with it into the mind's concepts—especially when what is true is loved, for everything true is in the light.[7]

Helen Keller did not let her blindness keep her from seeing. The heaven described in Swedenborg's writings was so vivid and real that she could not wait to get there:

> Heaven, as Swedenborg portrays it, is not a mere collection of radiant ideas, but a practical, livable world. It should never be forgotten that death is not the end of life, but only one of its most important experiences.
>
> In the great silences of my thoughts all those whom I have loved on earth, whether near or far, living or dead, live and have their own individuality, their own dear ways and charm. At any moment I can bring them around me to cheer my loneliness. It would break my heart if any barrier could prevent them from coming to me.
>
> But I know there are two worlds—one we can measure with

4. *HH*, p 312.
5. *HH*, p. 313.
6. *AC*, p. 448.
7. *HH*, p. 603.

line and rule, and the other we can feel with our hearts and intuition. Swedenborg makes the future life not only conceivable, but desirable.

His message to the living who meet the night of death with its attendant separation and sorrow sweeps across the heart of humanity like some sweet breath from God's Presence. We can now meet death as Nature does, in a blaze of glory, marching to the grave with a gay step, wearing our brightest thoughts and most brilliant anticipations, as Nature arrays herself in garments of gold, emerald, and scarlet, as if defying death to rob her of her immortality.[8]

To the late Reverend W. Cairns Henderson, a devoted student of Swedenborg, the vision was just as inspiring:

There is no more beautiful picture in the Writings of Swedenborg than that which portrays the life of heaven. In it, the angels are seen basking in perpetual spring. They dwell in gracious homes, beautifully appointed, and set in lovely surroundings unmarred by the presence of anything ugly or unclean. All their legitimate wants are supplied by the Lord without stint. Each is engaged in an absorbing task in which he forgets himself utterly; not to earn his daily bread, but because it is the work for which his mind most fits him, which above all he most wants to do, and in the performance of which he most truly fully lives.

In their societies, dwelling among those only who are like-minded with themselves, and with whom they most want to be, we see the angels living a full, well-balanced and gracious life, in which work, worship, social intercourse, and recreation each has its rightful place and its proper use and value. And we see them living a peaceful and happy life, in communities which are untroubled by friction, incompatibility, jealousy, envy, or unlawful desire; a life based upon mutual love, in which affection, respect and admiration for and appreciation of another's uses are expressed in sincere courtesy and goodwill, and in which conjugial love (perfect marriage love) makes possible a true love between the sexes. No anxiety, solicitude, or dissatisfaction mark their days; for they are satisfied with their lot and content in God.[9]

This vision may articulate the dreams about heaven of others who

8. Hellen Keller, *My Religion*, (New York: Swedenborg Foundation, 1953), pp. 203-4.
9. W. Cairns Henderson, *New Church Life* (pubished by the General Church of the New Jerusalem, Bryn Athyn, Pa.) March 1951.

wish for life without illness and ugliness, peace without threat of war and crime, perfect justice, the freedom to do what they most love to do, and the opportunity to do all they can for those they love. Many would love to be forever free of anxiety about the needs of this world.

We are told, "Seek ye first the kingdom of God and His justice, and all these things shall be added unto you."[10] But how do we seek the kingdom of God in a world so caught up in the here and now?

"A heaven-bound life," Swedenborg writes, "is not a life withdrawn from the world, but a life involved in the world." This is not a life of isolation and meditation. "It is a life of charity, a life of behaving honestly and fairly in every task, every transaction, every work, from a more inward source, hence a heavenly one."[11]

Choosing heaven simply means making it part of your life on earth. It is living a heavenly life that makes heaven life's natural fulfillment. It wouldn't make sense to expect to go to heaven after living a life opposed to it. You not only wouldn't deserve it, but couldn't possibly be happy there. "Every single person is born for heaven—accepted if he accepts heaven into himself in the world, and shut out if he does not."[12]

We are told that the life that leads to heaven is not difficult. But the life that leads to hell can be almost too easy if we let the hellish influences in us lead us there. Hell is the home of evil. But evil can be a subtle thing as well as blatant. Swedenborg describes the evil of hell in general terms as any selfish feeling that turns away from God. That can mean murder or just everyday unkindness.

People who choose hell do so by rejecting God in their lives; by doing what they know is wrong and justifying it as right; by putting their own needs above those of everyone else; and by being adulterous, deceitful, cruel or hateful, without conscience and without any desire to reform.

Swedenborg's picture of hell is as disturbing as his vision of heaven is inspiring. Hell is not a place of never- ending torture in burning pits. But it is an eternal world of frustration and torment, hatred and revenge, deceit and cruelty. There is no thought of being kind to one another. The inhabitants of hell live for themselves alone.

Swedenborg says there are hundreds of thousands of colonies in hell—some mild, some severe, and a lot in between. To those in hell, it is a normal enough world because it reflects everything they love. To those in heaven, hell is an incredibly repulsive place. But the people in hell are content and would live nowhere else, because nowhere else could they indulge the lifestyle that brought them to it.

Death is the ultimate equalizer in life. There are no VIP gates into

10. Matthew 6:33.
11. *HH*, p. 535.
12. *HH*, p. 420.

heaven. But there is a gate for everyone who truly wants to enter. You would think that everyone would line up at those gates. But Swedenborg says there are none so deluded and sad as those who suppose that given the ideal surroundings of heaven they could change the pattern of their lives overnight and be happy there. You will enter the spiritual world the same person you are when you leave this world. If there is any changing to be done, it has to start here.

The message that comes through the writings of Swedenborg is that your spiritual life is not something that begins when you die. It starts the moment you are born into this life. All of your natural life determines what its spiritual fulfillment will be. And that is what gives your life its meaning—the choice.

2

Swedenborg—Man beyond Measure

To my mind, the only light that has been cast on the other life is found in Swedenborg's philosophy. It explains much that was incomprehensible.
—**Elizabeth Barrett Browning**

Who is Emanuel Swedenborg?

The Schaff-Herzog *Encyclopedia of Religious Knowledge* considers him "in many respects, the most remarkable man of his own or any age."[1]

Ralph Waldo Emerson called him "a colossal soul who lies vast abroad on his times. He is not to be measured by whole colleges of ordinary scholars."[2]

Edwin Markham, the American poet known for his *"Man with the Hoe"* and *"Lincoln, the Man of the People,"* said, "There is no doubt that Swedenborg was one of the greatest intellects that has appeared upon the planet." He considered Swedenborg "the wisest man in millions. He was the eyeball on the front of the 18th Century."[3]

Helen Keller, a remarkable woman in her own right, whose book *My Religion* is a song of praise to the writings of Swedenborg, called him a "Titan Genius."[4] To her he was "an eye among the blind, and ear among the deaf."[5] And he emerged, in her special sight, as "one of the noblest champions Christianity has ever known."[6]

Who is this man so revered by other intellects? Who is this man con-

1. The New Schaff-Herzog *Encyclopedia of Religious Knowledge.* (New York: Funk and Wagnalls, 1808-12).
2. Ralph Waldo Emerson, chap. 3 in *"Representative Men,"* "Swedenborg or The Mystic," (London: Underwood, 1896).
3. "Swedenborg, a Colossus in the World of Thought," *The New York American,* 7 Oct. 1911.
4. Helen Keller, *My Religion.* (New York: Swedenborg Foundation, 1953), p. 2.
5. Ibid., p. 17.
6. Ibid., p. 25.

sidered to have one of the highest IQs in history? Who is this man with more expertise in more fields than any scientist before or since? Who is this man who left the largest collection of theological writings known in the world?

During his lifetime, Swedenborg's contributions to science, philosophy, and theology were well known in European intellectual circles. Among those acquainted with him or his published works were Immanuel Kant, Carolus Linnaeus, John Wesley, King Charles XII of Sweden, Goethe, Rousseau, and Voltaire. This was an age of remarkable enlightenment and genius, including such other contemporaries as George Washington, Frederick the Great, and Johann Sebastian Bach. Some reacted favorably to Swedenborg's theology, others argued with it; but just about every leading thinker of this age took note of it.

Swedenborg was a hard man to ignore. He was not only a leading scientist and philosopher but an esteemed member of the Swedish House of Nobles, a respected economist, an inventor, and a scholar. And all of this came before the most remarkable period of his life as revelator and "servant of the Lord"—a calling to which he took with humble commitment.

That was the time in his life that separated him from other renowned men, because of his unique spiritual experience. Between 1720 and 1745 Swedenborg had already written some twenty large volumes on civil, scientific, and philosophic subjects. Then, beginning at age fifty-seven and continuing for the last twenty-seven years of his life, he wrote thirty volumes of painstakingly thorough theology, plus a five-volume *Spiritual Diary*.

Swedenborg's fame did not die with him, nor was it confined to the European intellectual community. Many leading thinkers in the nineteenth century continued to recognize him as a man of exceptional insight. Among those acknowledging that their thinking was affected by his theology were Abraham Lincoln, William Blake, Robert and Elizabeth Barrett Browning, Thomas Carlyle, Samuel Taylor Coleridge, Edward Everett Hale, William Dean Howells, Jean Oberlin, and John Greenleaf Whittier.

Now the twentieth century, an age of technological marvel and materialistic focus, seems hardly aware of Swedenborg's science, philosophy, or theology. Most of his writing was done in Latin, which translates into stilted English and does not make for easy reading. But those thirty volumes of theology are closely reasoned and strikingly relevant. Swedenborg deserves to be known better.

Emanuel Swedenborg began his life in Stockholm, Sweden, on January 29, 1688, as the son—the third of nine children— of Jesper and Sara Swedberg. His was an intensely religious family. Most of the children were given scriptural names to remind them of their duty to God and the church. Emanuel means "God with us."

Jesper Swedberg was professor of theology at the University of Uppsala and dean of the cathedral there. He later became bishop of Skara, which made him a nobleman and caused the family name to be changed from Swedberg to Swedenborg. He served as chaplain to the royal family of Sweden, which led him into the highest social and political circles in the land. His wife's family was also prominent in Sweden's important mining industry.

The Swedenborg home was genteel and reverent. Even though Emanuel's mother died when he was just eight years old, her soft nature was to have an effect on him throughout his life. He grew up listening to discussions of religious questions and classical subjects, and eagerly joined in. Exchanging ideas about life and faith with a variety of clergymen helped him to develop his own philosophy. Near the end of his life he confided in a letter to a friend that during his formative years, "I was constantly engaged in thought upon God, salvation, and the spiritual diseases of men."

When he was just eleven years old, Emanuel entered Uppsala University, which was not unusual for a boy of high intellectual promise of that time. The university offered four major fields of study: theology, law, medicine, and philosophy. His inquiring mind was not content to settle on just one. He majored in philosophy, which included science and mathematics, but also took courses in law, and later proved himself learned in theology and medicine.

Most of his instruction was carried on in Latin. He learned it so well that he wrote poetry in Latin for relaxation. He added Greek and Hebrew, and when he began to travel, also learned English, Dutch, French, and Italian. He studied music on the side and filled in for the church organist. As a student, he was as versatile and curious as he was thorough and practical.

He completed his formal studies at age twenty-one, but his quest for broad learning hardly had begun. In a time when few men became really learned, he spent the first thirty-five years of his life in a massive program of formal and self-directed education. Within a year of leaving the university he was traveling in England, studying physics, astronomy, and most of the other known natural sciences.

Emanuel was also inclined to practical mechanics, a field often foreign to the intellectual. He became skilled in watchmaking, bookbinding, cabinet work, engraving, and the construction of brass instruments. Later, in Holland, he studied lens grinding—then an infant science. Further studies included cosmology, mathematics, anatomy, physiology, politics, economics, metallurgy, mineralogy, geology, mining engineering, and chemistry.

Swedenborg was not just a professional student. He was always trying to put his learning to work. And he never stopped thinking beyond what he learned. He was the first scientist to propound a nebular hypothesis—a theory of the formation of the stars and planets from a rotating nebular mass. He also founded the science of geology in Sweden and carried on exhaustive work in metallurgy.

This was just the beginning. His discoveries founded the science of crystallography. He followed the pioneer work of Sir Isacc Newton to discover more about the nature of magnets. And he anticipated Einstein's theory of energy by postulating an elaborate theory of his own about the source of energy, with similar conclusions.

Swedenborg made a feasible model of a glider-type airplane, almost two hundred years before the Wright brothers, and a model of a submarine long before anyone else saw the possibility. He made the first mercurial air pump, invented a stove that became widely used, improved the ear trumpets then in use (winning the praise of the deaf), anticipated the phonograph by creating a musical machine, designed a machine gun, and marketed a fire extinguisher.

He plunged into anatomy with the same curiousity and initiative. This was still a primitive science in Swedenborg's day. Neither the complete circulation of the blood nor the existence of oxygen were known. Even the functions of the heart and lungs were not clearly understood. Swedenborg not only came closer to perceiving these functions than anyone to that date, but was ahead of his time in many other areas of anatomical research.

He had devoted two years to anatomical research in Paris in the middle-1730s and produced one of his most famous philosophical books, *The Economy of the Animal Kingdom.* He made important discoveries about the brain, including functions of the motor areas, the ductless glands, and the circulation and uses of the cerebrospinal fluid. His studies of the nervous system and the brain are credited as the first accurate understanding of the cerebral cortex and the respiratory movement of the brain tissues. Modern scholars concede that Swedenborg's findings pointed the way to most of the fundamentals of nerve and sensory physiology.

Throughout this intense period of study and accomplishment, Swedenborg never forgot the advice of his father: "I beg you most earnestly that you will fear and love God above all else, for without this fear of God all other training, all study, all learning is of no account."

His life was not spent indulging personal and intellectual whim, however. He was also devoted to public service, to the Swedish government and its industry. As an already acclaimed scientist at age twenty-eight, he was appointed by King Charles XII as extraordinary assessor in the Royal Board of Mines. That sounds like a title with more pomp than obligation, but it made him responsible for the supervision and development of mining, then one of Sweden's most important industries. He took the job seriously, serving for thirty-one years.

He spent most of seven summers traveling on horseback and in carriages around the country, inspecting mines for safety and preparing detailed reports on the quality and amount of ore being mined. He was also involved in personnel and administrative decisions, arbitrated labor disputes, made suggestions for mining improvements, and collected national taxes levied on mining. And conscientious as this service was, he still managed leaves of absence for travel and study to further broaden himself and prepare for greater work to come.

His public career also included some fifty years of service in the House of Nobles, one of the four estates of the Swedish Riksdag (legislature). He was deeply devoted to the welfare of his country and carefully planned his travels for periods of legislative adjournment. He frequently wrote pamphlets and resolutions on pressing issues, from the economy and tax structure to foreign policy and development of Sweden's natural resources. He never shied from critical debate but was always a man of moderation, willing to work toward practical solutions.

Among his contributions was a system for amortizing mortgages along with interest payments, which only became common practice in this country in the past few decades. He also made significant contributions by putting his mechanical genius to work for his country. King Charles was so impressed by his leadership as editor of the first scientific journal published in Sweden that he asked him to serve as engineering advisor. Swedenborg supervised construction of several major public-works projects, including designing a dry dock, a canal, and a system for moving large warships over land.

In spite of his success in so many fields and the temptation he must have felt to devote himself to metallurgy or biology, he resisted extensive research because he didn't feel particularly gifted or suited to it. He became more interested in generalizing from the findings of others than conducting extensive experiments on his own. To him, what could be done with these findings was more important than his own fame.

Swedenborg had two main philosophic interests: cosmology, which is the study of the origin and order of the universe, and the nature of the human soul. For twenty-five years, between 1720 and 1745, while engaged in a host of other interests, he immersed himself in wide-spread study and writing on these sujects.

A six-hundred-page manuscript detailing his philosophy about the creation of the universe and what keeps it going was published posthumously. It stated his primary conclusion about matter, based on a "first natural point." This point, he theorized, was caused by Divine impulse and consists of pure motion, expanding by degrees throughout creation. His view of cosmology was teeming with energy. And modern research, particularly in atomic energy, has confirmed many of his theories. Svante Arrhenius, Nobel Prize winning chemist and founder of the twentieth-century science of physical chemistry, concluded that such "pioneers" as Buffon, Kant, Laplace, Wright, and Lambert all propounded theories of creation already suggested by Swedenborg.[7]

All of Swedenborg's work rested on the assumption that Divine force underlies all matters. He was not satisfied with purely material explanations of the universe. This led him to study both the relationship between the finite and the infinite, and the assumption that the human soul is the link between God and man.

He developed his search for the soul in a lengthy two-volume treatise, *The Economy of the Animal Kingdom,* which was praised by contemporary scholars. He pursued his search for rational explanations in anatomical research, which produced several additional books, some published, some left simply as manuscripts. Through it all he developed an amazing insight into the existence of the soul.

At age fifty-seven, with a seemingly full career behind him, he had gone as far as he could in attempting to explain the mysteries of human existence. He felt dissatisfied that his research had not provided a definitive answer. But he was about to begin that unique phase of his life that would take him deeper into understanding these mysteries than he ever could have imagined.

It began during 1744 and 1745 with a series of dreams an visions that profoundly affected him, leaving him sometimes fearful, sometimes exhilarated. Ever the scientist, he kept, in a *Journal of Dreams,* a careful record of what he experienced and how he felt about it. But this was a disquieting period, which he did not yet understand, so he kept the dreams to himself.

Swedenborg came to believe that he had been called by God to transmit a new revelation to the world, and he devoted himself to that service for the remaining twenty-seven years of his life. He began with a two-year study of the Bible, writing some 3,000 pages of personal notes and a complete Bible index, which he used extensively in writing his later theological works. He also perfected his Hebrew and Greek so that he could study the Bible in original texts.

From the time he began this spiritual mission, he claimed to have talked almost daily with spirits in their world, while he lived an apparently normal life among friends on earth. After a few years of this he wrote in *Arcana Coelestia* (Heavenly Secrets), "By the Divine mercy of the Lord it has been granted me now for some years to be constantly and continuously in the company of angels and spirits, hearing them speak and speaking with them in turn. In this way it has been given me to hear and see wonderful things which are in the other life, which have never come to the knowledge of any man."[8]

7. Svante Arrhenius, *Emanuel Swedenborg as a Cosmologist.*

Swedenborg insisted that what he saw and heard in the spiritual world came to him not in dreams but "in the highest state of wakefulness."[9] He was able to reflect on his experiences and write about them with real understanding. And he insisted that at all times he was taught by the Lord alone—*through* angels but not *by* angels.

In modern encyclopedias he often is identified as "scientist, philosopher, and mystic." But he cannot be so simply classified, because his experience was unique. It has nothing in common with the visions of self-styled seers, and in no way does he encourage a mystical way of life. For instance, he does not claim to have attained communion with God through contemplation, as many mystics do. He prayed to God but never consciously set out to commune with Him or spirits. First as scientist and then as philosopher, he sought an understanding of the soul as a link to God, not a beatific vision of God.

The revelation given through him contains nothing to help or encourage anyone to communicate with the spiritual world. Mysticism has no rational basis; the thirty volumes of Swedenborg's writings are an intricate presentation of thoroughly organized doctrine, free of rambling and contradiction. Some of his most pointed statements, in fact, are directed against those who try to communicate with spirits. In his stern warnings against blind faith, his theology openly discourages any inclination toward mysticism.

Also, unlike some self-professed revelators, Swedenborg did not rush into print the moment he felt called, nor did he try to attract attention to himself. In addition to the long preparatory work he did on earth, he waited until he had three years of experience visiting the spiritual world before he began to write.

In 1748 he launched his most exhaustive theological study, *Arcana Coelestia*. This twelve-volume work presents an analysis of the internal, spiritual meaning of the books of Genesis and Exodus, verse by verse and almost word by word.

Other books, some published posthumously, included *Divine Love and Wisdom; Divine Providence; The Four Doctrines* (The Lord, the Holy Scriptures, Life, and Faith), *Heaven and Hell; Conjugial Love* (a study of ideal marriage love), eight volumes explaining the Book of Revelation (two are *Apocalypse Explained* and *Apocalypse Revealed*), and *The True Christian Religion*.

In the beginning, he published his books anonymously, seeking no credit for them, even among friends. He invested a considerable amount of his own money. Distribution was quite modest at first, mostly anonymous gifts to clergymen, universities, and libraries.

8. *AC*, p.5.
9. *AC*, p.885.

He lived a normal life, if sometimes secluded, during the early part of this experience. He never married, which left him free to spend a lot of time with his books and studies. Friends and acquaintances noticed nothing unusual about his life.

Later experiences reversed this anonymous, secluded pattern. He became well known for something more than science and government service, and his books were widely read and discussed among learned men. Still he remained humbly committed to the conviction that he had been commissioned by God to bring this new revelation to the world. He never sought any personal acclaim.

It is interesting to note what he was *not* commissioned to do. He had no command to establish a church or found a religious movement, although he assumed that this revelation was to be the basis for a new church. This sets him apart from the Apostles, who were commanded to preach the Gospel. And it sets him apart from those who claim to have special insights and do all they can to attract a following.

Swedenborg was able to maintain his theological anonymity until 1759, when some amazing experiences occurred, bringing him considerable notoriety as word of them spread through Swedish society. This eventually led some readers to connect him with his unsigned books, particularly *Heaven and Hell*.

In July of 1759 he was attending a party with fifteen people at the home of a wealthy friend in Gothenburg, some 300 miles from Stockholm. Suddenly he became quite pale and disturbed and withdrew into the garden. He returned to tell his friends that a terrible fire had broken out in Stockholm, not far from his home. He was worried because the fire was spreading rapidly and he feared that some of his manuscripts would be destroyed. He was greatly agitated for several hours, but at last cried out, "Thank God! The fire is extinguished the third door from my house."[10]

That same evening, one of the guests present told the story to the provincial governor, who in turn asked for a full account from Swedenborg. The next day Swedenborg was able to describe the fire in some detail, including how it was put out, and this "news" quickly became the talk of Gothenburg. It was the following day—two days after the fire—that a messenger arrived from Stockholm with details that verified Swedenborg's account.

The interest aroused made him a pubic figure, and it wasn't long before it was known that he was the author of *Heaven and Hell* and *Arcana Coelestia*. Prominent people, anxious to meet a man who claimed to see into the spiritual world, began to write about him. Some who had not met him jumped to the conclusion that he must be insane, but those

10. Cyriel Odhner Sigstedt, *The Swedenborg Epic*, (New York: Bookman Associates, 1952), p. 269.

who did meet him were convinced of his mental stability because he was always calm, cordial, and rational.

While such a sensational experience attracted much more attention than the communication with spirits described in his books, it did arouse interest in the revelation he was transcribing and gave him a certain credibility.

A similar incident occurred the following spring. The widow of the Dutch ambassador in Stockholm became interested in Swedenborg's apparent ability to converse with spirits, and she approached him for help. A silversmith had presented a large bill for a silver service her husband had bought before his death. She was certain he had paid the bill but couldn't find the receipt.

A few days later Swedenborg reported that he had seen her husband in the spiritual world and had been told by him that he would send a message to his wife. Eight days later the lady dreamed that her husband told her to look behind a particular drawer in a desk. She did, and found not only the receipt but a diamond pin that also had been missing.

The next morning Swedenborg called on her, and before she could tell him what had happened, he told her that he had been talking to her husband the previous night and that her husband had left the conversation to convey a message to her.

Then in the fall of 1761, Swedenborg was invited to visit Queen Louisa Ulrika, who had become interested in his acclaimed abilities. The queen asked if he would communicate with her late brother Augustus William, who had died two years previously. A few days later Swedenborg returned and presented the queen with copies of his books. And in a private conversation he told her something that caused her to gasp in amazement, exclaiming that no one but her brother would have known what he had told her. This incident became widely known and discussed in Swedish social circles.

Swedenborg's fame quickly grew. One whose curiousity was aroused was the great German philosopher and rationalist Immanuel Kant. He never met Swedenborg but corresponded with him. And while he tended to discount anything spiritual, the persistent and authoritative reports about Swedenborg's experiences gave him pause. Sometimes Kant wrote favorably about Swedenborg, sometimes he was quite critical, but even his most searing criticism was pitted with doubts. Kant, like other intellects of his day, could not explain away Emanuel Swedenborg.

Friends and acquaintances who wrote of their impressions of Swedenborg, and even those who could not bring themselves to accept his claims would not say anything critical about him personally. He was described consistently as a gentle, humorous man with a relaxed, benign air.

When he was eighty, in excellent health and working on his last theological volume, *The True Christian Religion,* a friend wrote, "Someone might think that Swedenborg was eccentric and whimsical, but the very reverse was the case. He was very easy and pleasant in company, talked on every subject that came up, accommodating himself to the ideas of the company, and never speaking of his own views unless he was asked about them."[11]

A year later, in 1769, he was forced to answer charges of heresy leveled against him by some prelates of the Lutheran state church in Sweden. Friends had warned him that his theological writings had stirred considerable controversy in the Lutheran Consistory in Gothenburg. Clergymen and laymen were speaking out in favor of his theology, but others were strongly critical.

Earlier, in September of 1768, a country parson had brought debate in the Consistory to a head by introducing a resolution to stop the circulation of books not in line with official Lutheran dogma. The parson objected particularly to Swedenborg's theology.

While some members of the Consistory insisted that no decision should be made until all members had studied the books, the ranking prelate announced that he had found Swedenborg's doctrines to be "corrupting, heretical, injurious, and in the highest degree objectionable."[12] He confessed that he had not read any of the books closely, except *Apocalypse Revealed.* But still he charged Swedenborg with Socinianism—refusal to accept the divinity of Christ.

Swedenborg, whose theology emphatically teaches the divinity of Christ, wrote vigorously in his own defense. He said that he looked on the charge "as a downright insult and diabolical mockery."[13] The dispute raged on for several years, and the Royal Council finally imposed a ban on his books.

Swedenborg protested the decision and petitioned the king himself. The council referred the matter to the courts, which asked several universities (including Swedenborg's alma mater, Uppsala) to make a thorough study of his theology.

The universities asked to be excused because their theological faculties found nothing to condemn. But they were also reluctant to put bishops and consistories on trial for false accusation, which was the only way the issue could be reversed. The debate quieted down then, as the Consistory pursued no further action and some clergymen continued to preach Swedenborg's theology. Swedenborg himself continued to speak and write as he pleased.

He became engrossed in his last and crowning work, *The True Christian Religion.* At age eighty-two he undertook his eleventh and final foreign

11. Ibid., p.381.
12. Ibid., p.389.
13. Ibid., p.390.

20

journey to complete its publication. He must have felt he would not return, because he made farewell calls on friends and associates, arranged a pension for his faithful housekeeper, and settled his estate. He told a longtime friend and neighbor, "Whether I shall return again, I do not know, but this I can assure you, for the Lord has promised it to me. I shall not die until I have received from the press this work, now ready to be printed."[14]

Another somewhat skeptical friend visited him in Amsterdam during the printing and found him working on proofs "in an astonishing and superhuman way"[15] Swedenborg was convinced to the end that he rendered himself, as the title page of this final book stated, "The Servant of the Lord Jesus Christ."

He had predicted six months before his death that he would enter permanently the spiritual world on March 29, 1772—which turned out to be correct. He wakened from a long sleep that day after a period of poor health to ask his landlady and a maid for the time. When they told him it was five o'clock, he said, "I thank you. God bless you."[16] Then he gently sighed and died.

In the last month of his life several friends had urged that he make a final statement about the truth of the new revelation that had consumed his last twenty-seven years. But he answered pointedly, "I have written nothing but the truth, as you will have more and more confirmed to you all the days of your life, provided you keep close to the Lord and faithfully serve Him alone by shunning evils of all kinds as sins against Him and diligently searching His Word, which from beginning to end bears incontestible witness to the truth of the doctrines I have delivered to the world."[17]

To another friend shortly before he died he said, "As truly as you see me before your eyes, so true is everything that I have written; and I could have said more had it been permitted. When you enter eternity you will see everything, and then you and I will have much to talk about."[18]

14. Ibid., p.412
15. Ibid., p.415.
16. Ibid., p.433.
17. Ibid., p.431.
18. Ibid., p.432.

3

What Happens When You Die?

It is not death, it is dying that
alarms me.
—Montaigne

If babies had anything to say about it, they might be as fearful about birth as many of us are about death. The womb is their security. Life beyond it is unknown.

It is similar with our "rebirth" into spiritual life, when we pass from this world into the next. We may fear the end—which we call death and God calls birth—not knowing what comes next. But that "birth," like the first, is going to introduce us into a new life and a new world.

We get some encouragement about what it will be like to die from those who have reported the death experience to Drs. Moody, Kübler-Ross, and others. Almost all describe "a bliss before dying." None is afraid of facing death again. They have seen what it is like and call it "beautiful."

Swedenborg confirms their experience and goes considerably beyond. Those who are telling us what it is like to die give us just a glimpse. The consistency of the experience adds to their credibility, but still it is just a crack in the door. Swedenborg opens the door.

He begins with the assurance that you do not really die. You are simply separated from the body that served you in the world. The real you lives—"real" because it is not the body that is the real person but the spirit inside. Swedenborg notes: "For the spirit does the thinking in a person, and thought with affection constitutes the person. We can see from this that when someone dies, he simply crosses from one world into another. This is why 'death' in the Word, in its inner meaning, refers to resurrection and to continuity of life."[1]

The experience is described as so gentle that it is like waking from sleep. Even all the familiar surroundings of your last moment may be there still. You would have to be led, gently and in good time, to the realization that you had died and come into a new life. And at first it

1.*HH, p.445.*

may be hard to believe, because it looks so much the same. This may be a new world and a new life, but it is not going to be an unfamiliar place. It will be your spirit's home.

Swedenborg says that people often refuse to believe at first that they have died and come into another life, because it seems so much the same. "So much is this the case that when told he is a spirit, wonder and amazement possess him, both because he finds himself exactly like a man, in his senses, desires and thoughts, and because during his life in this world he had not believed in the existence of the spirit or, as is the case with some, that the spirit could be what he now finds it to be."[2]

Swedenborg tells of meeting a man who had just come into the spiritual world, who said he had believed in the existence of the soul "but had imagined that it must live after death an obscure kind of life, because if the life of the body were withdrawn there would remain nothing but what is dim and obscure. For he had regarded life as being in the body, and therefore he had thought of the spirit as being a phantom.... He now marvelled that spirits and angels live in the greatest light, and in the greatest intelligence, wisdom and happiness."[3]

What happens then when the soul leaves the body? Swedenborg was able to describe exactly how it feels to pass from this life into the next, because he was allowed to experience the sensation of death and resuscitation.

His physical breathing was "almost wholly taken away" while just the interior breathing of his spirit kept on. He was like this for several hours, aware of the presence of angels around him, when he became aware of "an aromatic odor like that of an embalmed body." It is this sphere, he says, that "keeps evil spirits away from a man's spirit when he is being introduced into eternal life."[4]

He said that "the angels first tried to discover what my thinking was, whether it was like the thinking of people who die, which is normally about eternal life. I also perceived that they wanted to keep my mind in that thinking. Later on, I was told that a person's spirit is kept in its last thought when the body dies, until it returns...." to the thoughts common to his life.[5]

Swedenborg describes how light comes gradually, as though the angels are rolling away a covering from the eyes. The light is bright but hazy, "rather like what a person sees through half-open eyelids when he first wakes up. At this point, the light seems to be a heavenly color, but then I was told that it varies."[6]

2. *AC*, p.320.
3. *AC*, p.443.
4. *HH*, p.449.
5. Ibid., p.
6. *HH*, p.450.

Then he felt something being gently rolled off his face, which was actually his awakening from natural to spiritual thought. "The angels take the greatest possible care to prevent the emergence of any concept from the awakened person unless it savors of love. Then they tell him that he is a spirit."[7] The angels do everything they can for those coming into their spiritual life, and begin to teach them about it. Those who aren't interested in learning about it want desperately to get away and are allowed to leave. But the angels never abandon them because "they love every individual, and want above all to be of service to him, to teach him, and to lead him into heaven."[8]

If a spirit turns away from them, "he is taken away by good spirits, who offer him all kinds of help as long as he is in fellowship with them. But if his life in the world was of a kind to make fellowship with good spirits impossible, then he craves release from them as well. This happens as long and as often as necessary until he joins the kind of spirits who wholly fit in with his life in the world, among whom he finds his kind of life. Then, remarkably, he leads the same kind of life he led in the world."[9]

This introduction to the life after death lasts only a few days, leading to the process of uncovering the true spiritual character that eventually brings each person, by his or her own choice, to heaven or hell.

Swedenborg tells of explaining to some people on the third day after their death that preparations were being made on earth for burying their bodies. They were struck with surprise, saying that they were very much alive and that what was being buried was only what had served them in the life of the earthly world.

> Later, they were quite amazed that while they lived in the flesh they had not believed in this kind of life after death, especially that almost everyone in the church shared this disbelief. People who have not believed, in the world, in any life of the soul after the life of the body, are acutely embarrassed when they realize that they are alive. But people who have convinced themselves of this opinion make friends with others of like mind and are separated from people who were in faith. For the most part, they are attached to a particular hellish community, because people of this worth have denied the Divine and despised the true elements of the church. In fact, to the extent that anyone convinces himself in opposition to the eternal life of his soul, he also convinces himself in opposition to the things that belong to heaven and the church.[10]

7. Ibid.
8. Ibid.
9. Ibid.
10. *HH*, p.452.

Some of those bound for heaven progress slowly and some quickly, some even immediately.

Swedenborg tells of one man who at first knew not where he was, supposing himself still to be in the world. But when he became conscious that he was in the other life, and that he no longer possessed anything, such as house and wealth, he was seized with anxiety and knew not where to betake himself, or whither to go for a place of abode.

He was then informed that the Lord alone provides for him and for all; and he was left to himself, that his thoughts might take their natural direction, as in the world. He now considered what he must do, being deprived of all means of subsistence. And while in this state of anxiety he was brought into association with some celestial spirits (angels from the highest heaven) who showed him every attention he could desire.

He was again left to himself, and began to think from charity (or good will) how he might repay kindness so great, from which it was evident that while he had lived in the body he had been in the charity of faith (meaning that he had lived his faith in a good life) and he was therefore taken at once into heaven.[11]

It's unusual though for anyone to go directly to heaven or hell. Most people spend weeks, months, years—even as much as thirty years—in this intermediate world, which Swedenborg calls the World of Spirits.

Through the centuries there have been a lot of theories about what happens between the time of death and the time that someone goes to heaven or hell. By relating his personal vision, Swedenborg illuminates what this place is and why we need it.

The first thing you learn is that you will find yourself after death in a world as real as the one you left, but with a lot of things you never have seen, heard of, or even imagined. You will see things in greater detail and brighter light. Your senses will be keener, your movements more effortless, your mind more active. You will be able to communicate much more clearly, to express all those thoughts that are so hard to put into words in this life.

You will still have your memory of everything from infancy to the end of your worldly life. That memory gradually fades as you enter more and more into your spiritual life, but it is important in the beginning that you keep this link with the world. Your memory is the foundation that connects your mental life into a cohesive identify, and it would be cruel if death suddenly wiped out everything you ever knew and had experienced. Your memory provides essential continuity from one life to the next, and will not let you escape the responsibility for your life.[12]

---

11. *AC*, p.318.

Your memory, of course, is not completely reliable, especially as you grow older. But that is your natural or "exterior" memory. You also have an "interior" memory, described by Swedenborg as "immeasurably surpassing the exterior" and upon which is impressed everything in your life—absolutely everything that you have said, thought, and done.

This is your "book of life" which:

> is opened in the other life, and according to which (you are) judged. Man can scarcely believe this, but it is most true. All the ends, which to him have been obscure, and all the things he has thought, together with everything that from these he has spoken and done, down to the smallest point, are in that book, and whenever the Lord grants, are made manifest before the angels as in clear day. This has several times been shown me, and has been attested by so much experience that not the least doubt remains.[13]

And he adds, somewhat ominously, "Let no one believe then that there is anything that a man has ever thought in himself or done in secret that can be concealed after death; but let him believe that all things and each single thing are then laid open as clear as day."[14]

This is not a time of anxiety, however, spent in acute embarrassment over all the secret things in your life suddenly revealed to others. For the most part these early days in the spiritual world are filled with happy reunions of wives, husbands, family, and friends, "who meet and converse together whenever they so desire."[15] This is part of the gentle introduction to this new life, in which God creates an atmosphere that best corresponds with each person's mental state.

How long you will stay here before finding your home in heaven or hell depends on how long it takes to separate what is good in you from what is not (and everyone has some of both), so that only what is dominant remains.

"For no one, in heaven or in hell," Swedenborg writes, "is allowed to have a divided mind"—to think one thing and do something else. Anything false or evil in people who are basically good is gradually replaced with heavenly truth and affections "that are appropriate for and fit in with their goodness." They become angels then, with nothing bad left in them.

The reverse is true with those who have chosen hell through their life and loves. What little of goodness or truth that they have affected to lend

12. Dr. Hugo Odhner, *The Spiritual World* (Bryn Athyn, Pa: Academy Publications Committees, 1968), p.100.
13. *AC*, p.2,473.
14. *AC*, p.2,488.
15. *HH*, p.73.

respectability to their lives leaves them, and they take on the nature that "fits in with their evil."[16]

Ralph Waldo Emerson said that "a man is what he thinks about all day."[17] Swedenborg confirms that what you choose to think about and love guides your life and makes you what you are. And underlying the complexity of all the things you love is that one pervasive and prevailing love, which Swedenborg calls your "ruling love"—the love that rules you.

This is your true character. It may be essentially good, leading to heaven, or intrinsically evil, leading to hell. You can never be absolutely sure in this life what your ruling love is. But you can have some idea just by reflecting on the things that please you most. This can be especially revealing. Consider what you choose to do when you are free to think and do as you like. It is not necessarily what comes into your mind in such moments that reveals your true character, but what you do with those thoughts, or would like to if you could.

The process that takes place in this World of Spirits is the uncovering of that ruling love so that your true character can be seen. This isn't going to take anything away from you, at least nothing that you don't want to be rid of. It will gently untangle the loose threads of your life into integrated patterns, so that it becomes clear to you what belongs to your character and what does not.

Swedenborg emphasizes that you determine your ruling love or basic character by your own free choice and follow it eventually to heaven or hell. And that character is fixed in you in this world and cannot change after death. Because what you love defines who you are, trying to love something else after death would contradict your life.

"I have been allowed to talk with some people who had lived two thousand years ago, people whose lives are described in histories and are therefore known. These people were found to be still the same, just like their descriptions, including the matter of the love which was the source and determining principle of their lives."[18]

In fact, your character comes to be seen in your appearance the more it is revealed. Those inclining to hell, with ugly personalities, appear in the light of heaven "crude, dark, black and misshapen"—although they may look lustily attractive to each other. Those with heavenly personalities appear "lively, bright, shining, and lovely." That all-defining love also shows in everything about them, from their clothes to the magnificence or squalor of their eventual homes.[19]

Let's take a closer look at what Swedenborg says you might expect as you pass through the World of Spirits to your final destination. A few

16. *HH*, p.425.
17. *The Complete Essays of Ralph Waldo Emerson.* (New York: Modern Library, 1940).
18. *HH*, p.480.

days after your resurrection, you would leave your first home, which might be almost a duplicate of the home you left on earth, and move on with other newcomers, with angels as guides. You probably would seek out the kind of people you liked to associate with on earth, settle down with them, and resume the normal habits of your life.

This is the first of the three successive stages after death described by Swedenborg. And it is the first experience that seems a little different from this world. You may be in it for only a few days, several months, or even up to a year. The length of time will depend on the harmony of what you show on the outside and what you really are on the inside. The closer those two sides of you are, the shorter the time spent in this stage. If there is no difference at all you might skip all the stages and be taken immediately into heaven, but Swedenborg says that is rare.

The second stage, as we have seen, is interior, inside your mind. Your spiritual body begins to reflect your mind and what it stands for, and this is especially seen in your face. The more in harmony you are with God and heaven, the more beautiful you become. If you are opposed to God and heaven, you grow progressively uglier.

The third stage is the final preparation for heaven, a time of instruction. Those who are going to hell need no preparation. They are ready for hell as soon as their evil nature is exposed in the second stage.

That second stage—the separation of your inward and outward characteristics to reveal the true you—is the most critical. It is also a fascinating process and one to make you wonder. You may feel like something of a Jekyll and Hyde in this life at times, hiding one personality behind what you show to the world. But you aren't unique or weird if you feel ambivalence in your own mind, with good instincts competing with nasty thoughts and evil urges. Everyone has some of that. You may wonder about "the real me" at times, and may welcome the discovery of who you really are, or be fearful of it.

Swedenborg notes:

> Every person has more outward and more inward aspects in his spirit. A spirit's more outward aspects are the means by which it adjusts the person's body to the world (especially his face, speech, and manner) for associating with other people. But the spirit's more inward aspects are the ones which belong to his own intention and resultant thought, which are seldom evident in the face, speech, or manner. From infancy, people get used to displaying friendliness and kindness and sincerity, and hiding what their own intentions think. So as a matter of habit they wear a moral and civic life in outward

19. *HH*, p.481.

matters, no matter what they are like inwardly. This habit is the source of man's virtual ignorance of what lies deeper within him, and also of his intentions to these matters.[20]

Once you know you are in the World of Spirits you will surely begin wondering if you are going to heaven. Most newcomers start out believing that they will, because they have lived outwardly moral lives. Even the worst among us on earth may live an outwardly admirable life: giving to charities, being good to neighbors, attending religious services, and cultivating a good public image. How often have you heard a slain crime figure eulogized as "a good man"? But that outer life you put on like your clothes may not show the real person at all. And it is that interior or real person who finds the home you already have made for yourself in heaven or hell.

In this life you easily can disguise your true feelings. In the other life it is impossible. This becomes acutely obvious during this second stage of spiritual development, as you reflect more and more the love that defines you. In this life we say that "the eyes are the mirror of the soul." In the spiritual life, the whole face, even the whole body, mirrors the soul. It really is impossible to assume a look contrary to your feelings.

The faces of hypocrites are changed much more slowly than others because they are so used to disguising their feelings. "However, since this imitative level is stripped off step by step, and the more inward elements of their minds are arranged in the form of their affections, later on they become more misshapen than other people."[21]

Swedenborg described the beauty of heaven as a reflection of the angels and the way their love of God and all that He stands for shines in their lives. "I have seen angelic faces of the third heaven, whose quality was such that no artist, with all his skill, could impart enough of that kind of light to his colors to capture a thousandth part of the light and life you can see in their faces. But the faces of angels of the lowest heaven can be captured to some extent."[22]

Progress in the World of Spirits from that worldly appearance to the interior world of the mind is a subtle process, just as you unconsciously slide from reality to daydreams in this world. "As a result, when the spirit-person is involved in this condition, he is involved in his very self and in his very own life. For thinking freely from his very own affection is a person's real life, and is the real person."[23]

As part of this process, your true character becomes more clear and pronounced than ever. If you have lived a life in harmony with God's

20. *HH*, p.492.
21. *HH*, p.458.
22. *HH*, p.459.

commandments in this world, you will live an even better life in the next. It is a life free of physical and psychological limitations as well as all the opposing influences that prey on you here. But those who are opposed to God are free of the restraints that may have forced the appearance of a good, upright life on them. Once their front is gone, their madness is unveiled.

Those who have tried to live a good life, who have acted from conscience, made an effort to shun what they understood to be evil, and made a place for God and His commandments in their lives, seem

> ... when they are brought into the condition proper to their more inward concerns, as though they have been roused from sleep and come awake, or have come from darkness into light. They are thinking on the basis of heaven's light, and therefore out of a deeper wisdom; they are acting on the basis of what is good and therefore out of a deeper affection. Heaven is flowing into their thoughts and affections with something more deeply blessed and pleasant, that they had not known about before.[24]

With those who live an evil life, who have no conscience, make no effort to resist what they know to be wrong, deny God, and have no place for religion in their lives, who live for themselves and the pleasures of the world, "they break out into crimes, contempt for others, acts of derision and blasphemy, of hatred, in vengefulness; they contrive plots, some so shrewd and vicious that it is almost impossible to believe that anything like them exists inside any person."[25]

Nothing about the real you is hidden when you come into this stage, especially your personal thoughts. There are none of the restraints that may check your words and actions in this life; concern about what others might think, fear of punishment, tarnished reputation, embarrassment, or other undesirable consequences.

Once your true character is uncovered, you can't disguise it and really would have no desire to. That is the real you. The secret things that are a part of you have to be dealt with openly. This is what is meant by God's words in Luke 12:2-3: "There is nothing covered up that shall not be revealed, and hid that shall not be known. Whatsoever you have said in darkness shall be heard in light, and what ye have spoken in the ear in the inner chambers shall be proclaimed on the housetops."

And in Matthew 12:36: "I say unto you, that every idle word that men

23. *HH*, p.502.
24. *HH*, p.506.
25. Ibid.

shall speak they shall give account thereof in the day of judgment."

That sounds threatening, doesn't it? Naturally there are parts of your life and thoughts that you would prefer no one even knew about. But this exposure of your inner thoughts is not a cruel and humiliating experience. It is a positive and essential part of the spiritual cleansing, something you have to begin in this life, if you are "choosing heaven," and complete in the World of Spirits. The further you get here in that cleansing, or change, the less that will have to be done there.

The focus is not embarrassment over things that you may regret having said, done, or even thought, but is on getting most of that unwanted aspect out of your life. It is a gentle and loving process, which forever frees you from all those hellish influences and eventually leads you to heaven. After all, God knows alls these things about you and never stops loving you. And it is that perfect love that pervades this cleansing process.

If you are headed for heaven, this process marks the beginning of the third and final stage in the World of Spirits, a time of preparation and instruction.

You have your own ideas of what is right and what is good, what is fair and what is honest, on a moral and civil plane, because there is a system of laws and the principles of your own faith to teach and lead you. But what is true and good on a spiritual plane can only be learned from God and heaven and has to be learned before you become an angel.

You can learn a lot of it from God's Word and from the various doctrines of faith drawn from it. But spiritual principles do not really become a part of your life, says Swedenborg, "unless in the more inward reaches of (your) mind (you are) in heaven."[26]

You are already in heaven in the spiritual, subconscious level of your mind when you recognize and acknowledge what is Divine and do what is fair and good and honest because that is what is commanded by your God and because it is what He loves in us and wants from us. It means acting justly and honestly in all things.

The more that you take the life of heaven into your life in this world, the less instruction you will need in the World of Spirits before entering heaven. But almost all who enter heaven need some instruction, which comes from specially prepared angels. And their backgrounds are always similar to those they instruct, so that they can relate closely to each other.

The instruction given to elevate you to heaven is "from doctrine drawn from the Word,"[27] accommodated to your level of understanding. The spiritual life begins with a moral life based on the principles you lived by in the world.

This instruction is different from what you were used to, because its

26. *HH*, p.512.

principles are not committed to memory as in your worldly life, but are applied directly to your spiritual life in the World of Spirits.

Swedenborg notes that with those being instructed after death "an affection for what is bonded to an affection for useful activity within every individual, so that they act as one."[28] Simply knowing about God and heaven does not bring you into heaven. It also takes a useful life based on that knowledge and a genuine love of it.

> There were some spirits who in the world had, by thinking, convinced themselves that they were going to enter heaven and be accepted in preference to others because they were learned and knew a great deal out of the Word and the doctrines of various churches. So they believed that they were wise, and were the ones meant by the people described as 'shining like the radiance of the firmament and like the stars (Daniel 12:3).' But they were examined to see whether their insights dwelt in their memories or in their lives.[29]

The Bible is filled with admonitions that you will be judged and rewarded after death according to your "works and deeds"—not just what you know, but what you have done with what you know.

Those who aren't living good lives may doubt that. They prefer to believe that everyone will be saved and taken into heaven out of pure mercy. But Swedenborg says, "When the Lord foretells the Last Judgment, he examines nothing but works, and He states in Matthew (25:32-46) that people who have done good works will enter life and people who have done evil works will enter condemnation... We can see that works and deeds are a person's outward life, and that the quality of his inward life takes visible form through them."[30]

This is because everything you do is an expression of your thought and will, which gives a uniquely personal dimension to every act, no matter how routine. Much more important than the acts, however, are the motives behind them. It is your motives—not what you do but why—that define your true character.

It is often as difficult to know your motives as it is to know the true you or the ruling love within you. You may feel your motives are generally good. But we all know that at times in our lives we act for less than noble reasons. This does not mean there is no hope, only that you cannot enter

27. *HH*, p.516.
28. *HH*, p.517.
29. *HH*, p.518.
30. *HH*, p.471.

heaven until everything impure or false has been uncovered and re-moved.

That is not easy, because a natural inclination for many is to cling to what they believe, even if it turns out to be untrue. Swedenborg notes that there are many who "from simplicity and ignorance have imbibed falsities of religious belief, and yet have a kind of conscience in accord-ance with the principles of their faith, and have not like others lived in hatred, revenge and adultery."[31] They cannot enter heaven yet, because those false beliefs have to be replaced with heavenly truth. So they remain in the World of Spirits for as long as this takes. The length of their stay and the intensity of the experience depends on how attached they are to those false beliefs.

Some are said to be almost eager to be cleansed for heaven. And they are encouraged by the angels that they eventually will be taken up into heaven. Whatever the discomfort of having to come to grips with the baser aspects of your character—and getting rid of them—the sphere pro-vided by the Lord and the angels is one of tender love and protection.

Once potential angels have been prepared for heaven through cleans-ing and instruction,

> they are dressed in angelic clothes, most of which are white like linen. (Then) they are brought to a path that heads up toward heaven and are committed to angel guardians there. Then they are accepted by some other angels and introduced into communities and there into many forms of happiness. Each angel is then taken by the Lord to his own community... When they arrive at their communities, their more inward reaches are opened, and since these are suited to the more inward reaches of the angels who are in that community, they are recognized immediately and accepted with joy.[32]

What happens when you finally leave the World of Spirits to make this ascent into heaven, or the descent into hell? Swedenborg describes this intermediate world as appearing

> ...like a valley among mountains and cliffs, with dips and rises here and there. The doors and gates to heavenly com-munities are not visible, except to people who have become ready for heaven; other people do not find them... The gates

31. *AC*, p.1,106.
32. *HH*, p.519.

and doors to the hells are not visible except to the people who are about to enter; for these people they are opened. Once they are opened, one can see dark, sooty-looking caves, leading down on a slant into the depth. . . . [3]

---

33. *HH,* p.429.

4

Heaven or Hell?– "The Country of the Heart"

I believe that men weave in their own lives the garment they must wear in the world to come.
—Abraham Lincoln

The biggest decision you make in your life is the one you live with forever: whether you will go to heaven or hell after death. You may never be aware that you are making the choice. And you may like to think that once the time comes you will just pick the path that leads to heaven and live happily ever after. But that, says Swedenborg, is not the way it works.

Long before you reach that point, you already have chosen the "gate" to your eternal life. The way you choose to live your life on earth leads you to the only place in heaven or hell that can be home for your spirit. It is what Helen Keller calls "the country of the heart."

The clear message in Swedenborg's writings is that everyone is born for heaven and no one is born for hell; that through our lives God is trying constantly to raise each of us up to heaven; and that every one of us can go to heaven if that is what we really want. Obviously, not all will want to.

Those who come into heaven are those who have allowed heaven to come into their lives on earth. Heaven is not a reward for a good life, it is the fulfillment of what already has begun to grow in you. The same is true in hell: it is not punishment for an evil life so much as the home for those who have made hell their lives. The potential for both is in you from the beginning. And the choice is always yours to make— every day, right now.

How do you let heaven come into your life while living on earth? It requires more than simply having a religious faith: it is really living that faith. When Jesus warned in His Sermon on the Mount that not everyone who called Him "Lord, Lord" would enter into the kingdom of heaven, "but he that doeth the will of My Father which is in heaven,"[1] He gave us the key.

To do "the will of My Father" is to live the way He wants us to live. That means especially obeying His commandments, with a real feeling for them, not just because it is the thing to do and be known for. Trying to live this way—even if it sometimes feels like a two-steps-forward-and one-step-back process as you wrestle with the temptations in your life—begins to bring you into heaven while still living on earth, because it introduces the real life of heaven into your mind. It is not enough simply to say you believe: you have to show that you believe by living what you believe.

If you "make your bed in hell," you also do it here. You do it by turning away from the heavenly life of loving and helping others and choosing instead a life that indulges and justifies selfishness, greed, adultery, deceit. It is certainly not what God wants for us, but it is what those who want it for themselves choose for themselves.

The idea that you choose heaven or hell during your life on earth, and that you can't change your mind after death, may be hard to accept. It challenges what for some is an instinctive notion that getting into heaven is simply a matter of believing in God and making the right choice when the time comes. But you can go only where your love directs you, because you can be content only where you can live with that love.

It would be easy for God to let you and everyone else into heaven, without your free choice entering into the matter. But that would not guarantee that you would be happy there. It also would take away your freedom, and that would destroy you as an individual. God wants you to choose heaven, but He will not interfere with your freedom to choose hell, if that is what you really want. That does not contradict the image of a loving God who draws all people to Him. It is the ultimate of love to let you be completely free to choose your life for yourself, including heaven or hell.

Swedenborg writes:

> Spirits who come from the world into the other life want nothing more than entrance to heaven. Almost all of of them request it, believing that heaven is nothing but admission and acceptance. So, since they desire this, they are taken to a particular community of the outmost heaven. For people who are involved in the love of self and the world, as soon as they

1. Matthew 7:21.

reach heaven's first threshold, they begin to hurt and feel so deeply tormented by pain that they feel hell rather than heaven within themselves. So they dive down headlong from the place, finding no rest until they are in hells with their own kind of people.[2]

He also notes that those from hell to whom he was allowed to talk were unanimous about one thing: "That they would a thousand times rather live in hell than out of it."[3]

But, "if people have not been taught about heaven, the way to heaven, and the life of heaven within man, they hold the opinion that acceptance into heaven is simply a matter of the mercy which belongs to people who are involved in faith, for whom the Lord intercedes. So they think that admittance is simply out of grace, and therefore that no matter how many people it means, all can be saved out of good will."[4]

Salvation—defined by *Webster's Dictionary* as "the saving of man from the spiritual consequences of sin"—and elevation into heaven depends on more than God's mercy and grace. His mercy is constant and directed "toward the whole human race, to save it, and it is also unceasing toward every man, and is never withdrawn from anyone, so that everyone is saved who can be saved.

The only way anyone can be saved is by Divine means, which have been revealed by the Lord in the Word. Divine means are called Divine truths. They teach how a person is to live in order to be saved. Through them, the Lord leads the person to heaven, and through them He endows him with heaven's life. The Lord does this for everyone; but He cannot endow anyone with heaven's life unless the person refrains from what is evil, because what is evil forms an obstruction.[5]

But before the door can fully be opened to let heaven flow into your life, you have to close the door to hell and shun its influences. Only after cleansing can healing begin. This is why so many of the commandments begin, "Thou shalt not . . .." You can't choose heaven without making a sincere effort to turn away from what is commonly considered to be a sin. And as you make the effort to resist what you know to be wrong, no matter how many times you have to start over, and try to live a good life from conscience, you will be led by God toward heaven.

Swedenborg writes that "the angels kept insisting that they had not yet seen anyone who had lived evilly accepted into heaven out of direct mercy, no matter how much assurance or confidence he had talked with in the world."[6] But that does not mean he can't be saved, just that he

2. *HH*, p.400.
3. *SD*, p.5,830.
4. *HH*, p.521.
5. *HH*, p.522.
6. *HH*, p.526.

cannot be saved without making the effort to be saved.

"I can testify from an abundance of experience that it is impossible to endow with heaven's life people who have lived a life opposed to heaven's life in the world. There were some people who believed that they would readily accept Divine truths after death when they heard them from angels— that they would believe and would live differently, and that as a result they could be accepted into heaven."[7]

> This was tried with some people who ...understood the truths and seemed to accept them. But the instant they turned back to their love's life, they rejected them; in fact, they spoke against them .... some wanted the love's life they had acquired in the world to be taken away from them, and an angelic life poured in its place. Even this was done for them, by special permission; but when their love's life was taken from them, they lay like corpses .... From these and other kinds of experience, straightforward good folk are taught that there is no way to change anyone's life after death; by no stretch of the imagination can an evil life be rewritten into a good one, or a hellish life into an angelic one. This is because every individual spirit is from head to toe of the same quality as his love—his life, that is— and changing this into its opposite would mean the complete destruction of his spirit.[8]

That may make heaven seem hopeless, when we know we are so far from being perfect. But the constant message of the Bible, reinforced throughout the writings of Swedenborg, is that is is not hard for anyone to get to heaven who really wants to be there.

You may have the idea that it will be hard because you must renounce the world and its pleasures, turn away from the "lust of the flesh," and take up a life of prayer and meditation. But Swedenborg writes:

> People who renounce the world and live by the spirit build up a mournful life for themselves, one that is not receptive of heavenly joy; for everyone's life awaits him. On the contrary, if a person is to accept heaven's life, he must live in the world, involved in its functions and dealings. Then through a moral and civic life he receives a spiritual life. This is the only way a spiritual life can be formed in a person, or his spirit prepared for heaven.[9]

---

7. *HH*, p.527.
8. Ibid.

The spiritual life is not something separate from your conscious life, but is joined with it as the soul is joined with its body. If separated it would be like a house without its foundation, because the conscious life is what gives expression to the spiritual life of conscience. They come together in what we call "living a good life."

Anyone can go through the motions of living a good life—-appearing just, honest, and generous. The difference with spiritual people is that they believe in God and try to live by what they accept as God's law, not just the expectations of civil and moral law.

The life that leads to heaven, Swedenborg writes, is not a life withdrawn from the world but a life involved in the world, (and) a life of piety without a life of charity (which occurs only in this world) does not lead to heaven. Rather, it is a life of charity, a life of behaving honestly and fairly in every task, every transaction, every work, from a more inward source, hence a heavenly one. This source is present in that life when a person behaves honestly and fairly because it is in keeping with Divine laws. This life is not hard. Rather, the life of piety withdrawn from a life of charity is hard. Yet this latter life leads away from heaven just as surely as people believe it leads to heaven.[10]

Swedenborg can say it is not difficult, but you know that it is not always easy. You may be encouraged about the course of your life one day and discouraged the next, as you struggle to overcome your weakness and elevate your life. This is the critical choice you make throughout your life: whether to follow a path separate from God or to follow God. Your instinct may be to depend more and more on yourself and the people you trust. But that is not what we are counseled to do in countless Biblical passages:

"Verily, I say unto you, except ye be converted, and become as little children, ye shall not enter into the kingdom of heaven. Whosoever therefore shall humble himself as a little child, that same is greatest in the kingdom of heaven."[11]

"Suffer the little children to come unto Me, and forbid them not; for of such is the kingdom of God. Verily I say unto you, whosoever shall not receive the kingdom of God as a little child, he shall not enter therein."[12]

Children are all innocence. They are dependent on their parents' leading. And spiritual innocence is a similar willingness to be led by God. This does not always come easily, even with those who consider themselves religious, and often your inclination may be otherwise. As you wander your own way, feeling lost at times, it takes some self- compulsion

9. *HH*, p.528.
10. *HH*, p.535.
11. Matthew 18:3-4.

if you really want to be led by God and what He stands for. But the harder you try, the easier it gets.

Jesus said in His Sermon on the Mount, "Blessed are the poor in spirit, for theirs is the kingdom of heaven."[13]Swedenborg says the "poor in spirit" are those who acknowledge that everything good in them and their lives really comes from God. The humble man is a teachable man, a man who can be raised up. But the illusion we live with is that we easily become wise enough for our own needs. It is an illusion we deeply cherish. But once we get past the illusion, we become "poor in spirit"—humble and heavenly— and thus spiritually rich.

Swedenborg says over and over that everyone can do this, that everyone who wants to go to heaven can turn his or her life and go there, no matter how wayward life may be; and that there is always spiritual hope and opportunity. Success is not inevitable and will not come without effort. But as long as you are seeking salvation and living for heaven, God and all of heaven are on your side. Those who do not seek heaven in this life will never find it in the other.

12. Mark 10:14-15.
13. Matthew 5:3.

5

The Heavenly Kingdom

*In my Father's house are many
mansions .... I go to prepare a
place for you.*
—John 14:2

What do we mean when we say something is "heavenly"? Usually those are the special moments that capture some of the promise of heaven: peace, pleasure, contentment, beauty, love. These are the moments we live for and never forget, moments that make heaven worth living for.

But for all that you long for relief from the trials of this world, heaven may seem vaguely intimidating. What will it really be like? Will you really like it there—forever? Or does the effect wear off and boredom set in? How big is heaven? Will it ever be filled? And will it ever be closed? Do angels sleep, work, eat, and live together as man and wife? This life is full of questions about that life— questions that usually do not have answers.

There are answers throughout the writings of Swedenborg, however, and those answers are consistently reassuring. Heaven is open to everyone who truly seeks it, he says. It will never be filled, never be closed. And it will never be boring. Heaven, after all, is a kingdom of love. And when you are doing what you really love to do, with and for people you love, you are blissfully happy and never think of being bored. This is the life of heaven.

Swedenborg's description of heaven does not sound that much different from the settings on earth we call "heavenly." But why should it? If it is where your love has led you, it is going to feel like home and look like home, not a strange and foreign place.

Swedenborg writes, "There are clouds, rain, winds, gravity, and other forces apparently like those of nature. There are greenswards, paradisal gardens, flowers and fields and fallowland, mountains and brooks, and even the seashore."[1]

1. Dr. Hugo Odhner, *The Spiritual World* (Bryn Athyn, Pa.: Academy Publications Committee, 1968), p.199.

There is also a sun shining constantly in heaven, and God is seen in that sun. Its light radiates His truth, its heat His love, creating a light described by Swedenborg as much brighter than our noonday sun, but not at all hard on the eyes.

That light is so penetrating that nothing is hidden from it. In that light you are seen for exactly what you are. This isn't threatening to the angels, though. They welcome this complete openness of their character, because by the time they have become angels there is nothing but good in them. They have nothing to hide, nothing of which to be ashamed.

"This is not the case with people who are below heaven and do not intend what is good. Such people have an intense fear of being seen in heaven's light. And strange as it seems, people in hell look human to each other, but in heaven's light they look monstrous, with frightening faces and bodies—they are the very models of their own evils."[2] In the light of heaven, angels are as beautiful as they are good; the more angelic, the more beautiful. And evil people are every bit as ugly outwardly as they have made themselves to be inside.

Swedenborg found it hard to describe what the angels see in heaven. Things do appear to be much the same as on earth, but their quality is so much finer and more perfect that they defy worldly terms.

He paints a general picture, but leaves you to stretch your imagination to glimpse the heavenly detail. There are "gardens and parks full of every kind of tree and flower. The trees are set in a very beautiful design, with arched entrances opening through, and with walks here and there. Everything is so beautiful that there is no way to describe it. ... There are kinds of trees and flowers there unknown in the world."[3]

That wouldn't be hard to get used to. What is going to take an adjustment, to our way of thinking, is a spiritual world without the limits with which we live in this world—time and space. Heaven doesn't have either. That is something almost impossible for us to understand, because almost everything we know is defined by space and time. But Swedenborg assures that this all will seem quite natural when you make the transition to a spiritual life, requiring no adjustment at all. We really are introduced into this spiritual world in our own minds, in dreams and imagination. For instance, we drift with daydreams to people and places near and far, without any relation to time and space. We may think of a friend far away and bring that person close. We can relive an experience from years ago and time disappears. So the experience of going beyond the limits of time and space will not be entirely new.

The spiritual world is not as different as we might think either. Most of us consider this a strictly structured world, with reality defined by

2. *HH*, p.131.
3. *HH*, p. 176.

what we can see and measure. But there is a lot that is very real to us that we can't see or quantify. For instance, you can't see or measure the love you feel for someone, but nothing is more real to you.

You know that even in the silence of your room there are radio waves and other forms of energy pulsing through the atmosphere, which become "real" only when transmitted to a wavelength we can hear or other wise sense.

Here on earth we are locked in to finite measurement, at least in the physical world outside our minds. But Swedenborg says, "people go utterly astray when they think this way about heaven. The expanse there is not like the expanse on earth. Here is a limited expanse and therefore measurable, there it is an unlimited expanse and therefore immeasurable."[4]

There is "distance" in heaven, of course—or at least the appearance of distance. Things and people are set apart, by greater and lesser degree. But that distance is not measured by constants, the way it usually is here. It is determined instead by changes in the angels' states of mind. If you feel distant from someone, you really are distant in the spiritual world. If you feel close, you will be together. That's because this is the spiritual world of the mind, not the purely physical world. But it is every bit as real to the angels as the tightly bound world of time and space is to earth's inhabitants.

Most of us depend on spacial relationships to define our world, but heaven is not so confined. When you want to go from one place to another here, usually you have to think of measurable distance and the time it will take to travel. But Swedenborg saw many times that angels will arrive at a place more quickly when they really want to be there and less quickly when the desire is less. He says that angels can't even think in terms of time and space, even though they lived with those limits in this world and still live in an environment of apparent distance and progression.[5]

Heaven is even more real than this earth, says Swedenborg, because in addition to the reality of the environment, love is seen clearly, and it is love that really makes up our own worlds. In the spiritual world of the mind, in this world and in heaven, everything in the mind is also part of the reality.

Probably the only way many of you can relate to this is through the free flow of your own thoughts, which float through your mind without anchors in time or space. Whatever you care to think about is right there in your mind, even though the scene or the person may be physically far removed. When you are lost in your dreams, time has no relevance, and space imposes no limits. And what you "see" and feel is real.

4. *HH*, p.85.
5. *HH*, p.195.

Apart from dreams and other suspended states in your mind, time rules your life in this world, and you can't help putting everything—even the life after death—in a time-space context. That might make the idea of living forever a bit unnerving, because of the endless passage of time. But you can't begin to understand eternity by thinking about it as time without end. Go back to your dreams, or when you are so engrossed in something that you don't put it on a time scale. Think of the times when you are happiest. Then time doesn't exist and you don't want it to end. You just live in that moment. And that is the eternity you have to look forward to: being totally caught up in a life that delights you, without any concept of time passing or time in the future.

Your life here is largely measured in degrees of time. The earth rotates around the sun, marking day and night, hours and seasons. But in heaven the sun is fixed, without any part of heaven oribiting around it, so that there is no obvious progression of time. But that does not mean it is always the same "time" in heaven, such as mid-afternoon. There is morning, afternoon, and evening there, "times" for work, recreation, worship, and rest, but only through changes in the state of mind, not absolute physical changes that can be measured by wristwatches.

Swedenborg says that the angels quickly lose all idea of time and just naturally take to a spiritual world reflecting changes in the mind—those internal changes that produce a corresponding environment. "They do not even know what is meant by the terms of time, such as year, month, week, day, hour, today, tomorrow, or yesterday."[6] And when you are harried in this world by the daily demands of time, doesn't that make heaven sound heavenly?

Lacking the constants of time and space that define much of our world, heaven may seem like a confusion of floating things and spirits. But Swedenborg describes it as a world of total order, just in a different context.

Heaven is divided into three levels: celestial, spiritual, and natural, each distinguished by the prevailing kind of love among the angels there. In the celestial, or highest, heaven, it is love of God that is paramount. In the spiritual or middle heaven, the dominant love is toward the neighbor, the love of helping other people. And in the natural, or lowest, heaven it is the love of obedience to the Ten Commandments and other Divine laws.[7] Each level of heaven is also divided into innumerable societies, according to "differences of love and faith" among the angels.[8]

When we make our friendships and association on earth, we do so primarily with people who share our interests and values. Angels similarly form their communities around common bonds. They are free to

6. *HH*, p.165.
7. *HH*, p.166.
8. *HH*, p.41.

visit among communities as they like, but it is in their own that they feel most at home and most free.

These societies may be large or small, their settings varying from country to city, but each is a community of its own. "The large ones are made up of tens of thousands of people, the smaller ones of thousands, and the smallest of several hundred. There are some people who live apart, home by home, and family by family."[9]

Heaven isn't going to put you in some foreign environment. If you love living in the country, that will be your heavenly home. And if you are most at home in a city or small town, you will feel comfortable in that kind of heavenly setting as well.

Because the angels in each society share common interests, it is not surprising that most angels in any one society are said to come from the same period in our history and often from the same country, although it is quite possible for angels from different periods and geographic areas to share the same basic interests and to dwell together. They live in the culture they are used to, but in a much more elevated state of mind. And the real distinction between societies is in the uses they perform, such as educating the young or instructing newcomers, rather than any sense of race, class, or nationalism carried from this world.

Swedenborg includes several descriptions of a heavenly community named for Athens, where ancient Greek philosophers live in the environment of that classical time. It is a large city with libraries, museums, and colleges, courts of justice, and a variety of businesses. He mentions their sports and games, the embroidery done by the women there, and the artistry "wrought by artisans in a spiritual manner."[10]

Individual homes reflect the personalities of their inhabitants. Your home on earth tells a good bit about you— what you care about and what you value. In heaven, this is even more the case. Every house is a gift from God, perfectly matched to every angel's character and personality.

In fact, your eternal home, whether in heaven or hell, will be so much a part of you that you will instantly recognize it as your own. This is because you are designing it and building it through the course of your life on earth. That house really will be home, forever.

That home will be part of a kingdom of perfect, peaceful order. Swedenborg describes a heavenly form of government: a sphere of mutual love extending from God down through the angelic societies. It is the kind of government many only could wish for on earth.[11]

It may be hard to imagine government without arguments and ego and with its people more interested in serving than ruling, but that is

9. *HH*, p.50.
10. *CL*, pp.75-77, 156a, 182, 207.
11. *HH*, p.213.

what makes this government heavenly. There the angels want only what is best for each other, so that governing there is quite different from what we are used to.

Swedenborg describes the officials there as:

> ... more than others involved in love and wisdom, the ones therefore who, out of love, intend what is good to everyone and who out of wisdom know how to provide that it happens. People like this do not domineer and give orders; they minister and serve .... They do not make of themselves more than others, but less, for they give first priority to the good of the community and the neighbor, and lower priority to their own good ....
>
> They do nevertheless have honor and glory. They live in the center of the community, higher up than others, and in splendid mansions. They do accept this honor and glory—not for themselves, however, but for obedience sake. Everyone there knows, in fact, that this honor and glory are given to them by the Lord, and that they are to be heeded on this account.[12]

Swedenborg also describes the government of hell, and the contrast tells all you need to know about the opposite natures of heaven and hell. Government is essential in hell, "for unless there were governments, the people there could not be kept fettered. But the governments involved are the opposite of governments in heaven. They all come under the heading of love of self. Everyone there wants to rule over others and to be on top. Given people who are not on their side, they hate them, wreak vengeance on them, and are violently hostile toward them, for this is what the love of self is like. As a result, the worst do the ruling, and are obeyed out of fear."[13]

---

12. *HH,* p.218.
13. *HH,* p.220.

6

The Life of Heaven

*It is not expected that the life
of heaven can ever be grasped
by natural thought, still less
described by out-ward features.
Yet these features, as given in
the Writings of Swedenborg,
are to be the basis of our
rational thought about the
other world.*
—Dr. Hugo Lj. Odhner, *The
Spiritual World*

Every heavenly moment in your life gives you a taste of what heaven is like all the time. But it can only be a glimpse, because what you call "heavenly" you see only in the context of this world. Heaven is a higher, spiritual plane. And while you may like to picture the peace, joy, contentment, and beauty there, Swedenborg says that you scarcely can approach any real idea of all it has to offer.

In your moments of greatest joy in this life it may be hard to imagine that anything could surpass such feeling. But Swedenborg insists that there is no comparison with the happiness of heaven.

Suppose that you were just coming into this new world. Swedenborg says that you would be introduced to it gradually, so as not to be overwhelmed. You might be taken first to "heavenly gardens beyond the most imaginative conceptions."[1] And while you begin to think, "this is it!" you are told that this is only the beginning.

You experience more and more "interior joy" until you arrive at a state of peace to the very core. Angels told Swedenborg that "nothing of this is expressible in any way or conceivable."[2] Finally you come to a feeling of innocence and purity that touches your inmost capacity for perception and sensation. And then you know, finally, what heaven is.[3]

1. *HH*, p. 412.
2. Ibid.
3. Ibid.

Most people come to heaven quite ignorant of all this. They suppose that heaven is a reward, "a kind of joy into which any can be admitted no matter how they have lived, even those who have borne hatred against their neighbor and have passed their lives in adulteries, being quite unaware of the fact that heaven is mutual and clean love, and that heavenly joy is the derivative happiness."[4]

You wouldn't think of moving to another country without learning all you can about its people, its customs, and its government. And Swedenborg says that you should be learning all you can about the place where you will go after death— where you will live forever.

> I have sometimes spoken with spirits fresh from the world concerning eternal life, telling them how important it was for them to know who is the Lord of that kingdom, and what is the nature and form of its government, just as those in this world who go into another kingdom are especially interested to know the kind of ruler, and what kind of government, and many other things which belong to the kingdom; and how much more they should be interested in this kingdom.
>
> I have told them that the Lord alone rules both heaven and the universe, and that the laws of the kingdom are eternal truths, all of which are based on the one great law that men shall love the Lord above all things and their neighbor as themselves, and now even more than themselves to be as angels . . . .
>
> (The love that is with the angels) finds its joy in being of service to others, not for the sake of self but for love's own sake. All this could not be comprehended by those who loved themselves more than others, and who in the bodily life had been greedy for gain.[5]

Swedenborg gives many vivid descriptions of people considered learned in this world who confess what they had imagined heaven would be like, and how they came to find how wrong they were—much to their relief.

He tells, for instance, of seven groups of angels called together to talk about what their ideas had been.

The first of these assumed that everyone would be admitted into heaven, no matter what kind of life he or she had led, and that everyone would join in the happiness, like guests at a wedding.

The second group envisioned "cheerful companionship with angels and sweet conversation with them"[6] to eternity.

4. *AC*, p.547.
5. *AC*, p.548.
6. *CL*, p.3.

The third said, "what else is heavenly happiness but feastings with Abraham, Isaac and Jacob, upon whose tables will be rich and delicate foods, with noble wines. And after the feasts, sports and dances of maidens and young men, tripping to the measures of tabors and flutes, with the sweet singing of odes. And then, at evening, dramatic presentations, and again feastings, and so on every day to eternity."[7]

The fourth group said that after considering the possibilities, they had come to the conclusion "that heavenly joys are paradisal joys. What else is heaven but a paradise of fruit trees and delightful flowers, in the center the Tree of Life, around which the blessed will sit, eating fruits of delicious flavor, and adorned with wreaths of the most fragant flowers."[8] They imagined that men and women would be "restored to the flower of their age, and thereby to the primitive state into which Adam and Eve were created, and so be led back into their paradise which has been transferred from earth to heaven."[9]

The fifth group saw heavenly joy and happiness as "supereminent domain and boundless wealth, with regal magnificence and illustrious splendor."[10] This they assumed from what had appealed to them in the world, and from the biblical promise that those in heaven will "reign with God."[11] They saw themselves as kings and queens, sitting upon thrones with angels attending to them, each with a palace resplendent with gold and precious jewels.

The sixth group felt that the joys of heaven "are nothing else than perpetual glorification of God, a solemn festival continuing to eternity, and most blessed worship, with songs and jubilees, and thus a constant uplifting of the heart to God."[12]

The last group consisted of angels who could not believe that there was such ignorance in the world about heaven. One of them explained that after death all men and women who had desired heaven and had some definite ideas about what it would be like were allowed to experience the "heaven" they imagined. When they learn that these imaginings are just "the vain ideas of their own mind and fantasy,"[13] and not at all what heaven is really like, they are led away and instructed.

This is just what happened with the first six groups of angels. They were allowed to experience exactly what they had imagined heaven to be—the feastings, the constant prayer, the power, wealth, and idleness—until they were sick of it and begged to leave.

7. Ibid.
8. Ibid.
9. Ibid.
10. Ibid.
11. Ibid.
12. Ibid.
13. *CL*, p. 4.

Chagrined by their mistaken beliefs, they asked an angel, "What then is heavenly joy?" And they were told, "It is the delight of doing something which is of use to oneself and others, and the delight of use springing from love is the soul and life of all heavenly joy."[14]

They were also told that companionship, recreation, and social life are all a part of heaven, but subordinated to the delight of being kind and useful to others. If that one essential joy is taken away, "the accessory joys become joyless, first indifferent, then like trifles, finally sad and distressing."[15]

Ten men who were invited from these groups to experience the real life of heaven came back to report on special days of festivity, with concerts, games, and songs. "Moreover, every morning, songs of utmost sweetness sung by young maidens are heard from houses around the public places, and the whole city resounds with them."[16]

This was followed by a peaceful stillness, as the angels went about their work. Later, children were seen playing in the parks and streets, including races and ball games, with laurel leaves awarded as prizes. They also mentioned theatrical performances and were invited to witness a wedding in heaven.[17]

The lesson they all learned is that while heaven has its diversions and special attractions, it is first a kingdom of usefulness. That is at odds with the popular notion of heaven as a place of perpetual leisure. But loving others and expressing that love by doing things for them is obviously more heavenly than an indulgent idleness that only serves self.

We feel some of that heavenly delight when we forget our own needs while doing things for those we love. But in this life many of us tend to attribute to ourselves any good that we do for others. In heaven, the angels know that everything good ultimately comes from God.

In fact, Swedenborg says, "angels attribute absolutely no credit whatever to themselves, refusing any praise or honor for what they do and crediting it to the Lord."[18]

The angels also "shake off any expressions of gratitude for good they have done. They are insulted and go away if anyone credits them with goodness. They are amazed that anyone would believe they are wise on their own or do good on their own. They do not call it 'good' when someone does good for its own sake, for this comes from the person himself. They call it 'good from the Lord' when someone does what is good for its own sake. Such 'good,' they say, is what makes heaven, because such good is the Lord."[19]

14. *CL,* p.5.
15. Ibid.
16. *CL,* p.17.
17. Ibid.
18. *HH,* p.230.
19. *HH,* p.9.

Angels avoid people who arrive in their world convinced that what they do is entirely from themselves. "They see them as senseless and as thieves" because they do not see God in the good things they do, and because they steal what is God's and make it their own.[20]

Swedenborg illustrates with the biblical teaching, "Abide in Me, and I, in you. As the branch cannot bear fruit of itself except it abide in the vine, so neither can you except ye abide in Me. I am the vine, ye are the branches. He that abideth in Me, and I in him, the same beareth much fruit; for apart from Me ye can do nothing."[21]

The delights of heaven are indescribable and innumerable. "But not one of these countless delights can be known or believed by a person who is involved in the pleasure only of the body or the flesh, because his more inward reaches are focused away from heaven and turned toward the world, that is backwards."[22] The pursuits of this world— honor, riches, and purely sensual pleasure—are so contrary to the delights of heaven that they suffocate the higher joys and destroy belief in them.

The difficulty is that the only good feelings we know are associated with life in this world; it is hard to imagine how much greater the happiness of heaven must be. Any sense of delight in loving God and the neighbor is often "only a blessedness that is almost imperceptible"[23] because it attaches more to the soul than to the body, and it is the body with which we feel most keenly in this life.

> But these situations change completely after death. Then the pleasures of love of self and the world are turned into things painful and fearful.... But the hidden pleasure, the almost imperceptible blessedness that existed within people in the world who were involved in love for God and in love toward the neighbor—this is then turned into the pleasure of heaven, perceptible and palpable in all possible ways. In fact, this blessedness that had lain concealed in their more inward parts while they lived in the world is then uncovered and released into open sensation, because then they are in the spirit and that pleasure proper to their spirit.[24]

Swedenborg describes some who had expected a nice, idle life, who were allowed to experience just that. "They felt that it was very gloomy, and that as all their joy vanished, they would become disgusted with it and sick of it."[25]

20. *HH* p.10.
21. John 15:4-5.
22. *HH*, p.398.
23. *HH*, p.401.
24. Ibid.
25. *HH*, p.403.

Others who anticipated a life of praising God were told He has no need for praise apart from a life that expresses it. "He rather wants people to perform useful deeds, that is, the good things that are called good works of charity."[26] The idea of constantly doing things for other people, instead of just relaxing and enjoying heaven, is not going to seem heavenly to those who live only for themselves. But the angels told Swedenborg that they feel most free and happy themselves when they are making others happy, instead of looking for reward.

But the real joy of heaven cannot even be described in terms of this life. Swedenborg says that "good spirits, who have not yet been promoted to heaven, when they perceive the delight from an angel because of the sphere of his love, they are filled with such delight that they fall into a kind of sweet swoon."[27]

If heaven so surpasses our expectations, what then of the angels?

Part of what makes that life so different from this is that angels never grow old. This is a life of the spirit, not the body. And while the spirit grows and progresses, it does not age.

> People who are in heaven progress steadily toward the springtime of life, and the more thousands of years they live, the more pleasant and happy the springtime. This goes on forever, with the increase keeping pace with the growth and level of their love, charity and faith. Women who have died aged, debilitated by age, who have lived in faith in the Lord, charity toward the neighbor, and happy, true marriage love with their husbands come more and more as years go by into the flower of youth and young womanhood—into a beauty that outstrips every concept of beauty that sight can possibly perceive .... In a word, growing old in heaven is growing young.[28]

The beauty of heaven, filled with angels wishing well and doing well for each other, creates a sphere of incredible bliss. The angels share their happiness in a harmony of joy. But that doesn't mean that heaven is always the same or that angels do not change their moods and attitudes. Their states of mind still vary, from inmost happiness to lesser feelings. Swedenborg saw both "the light and warmth of their life" and "shade and cold, or shrouded and unpleasant state."[29]

You might think that angels would always be "up." But Swedenborg was told that there are reasons why they are not. The delight of living in heaven would lose its appeal, for instance, if they were always in the

26. *HH*, p.404
27. *HH*, p.409.
28. *HH*, p.414.
29. *HH*, p.155.

same environment and state of mind. You know what that's like. Anytime you indulge in whatever pleases you, be it golf or gardening, skiing, or reading, you can't keep at it long without needing change. The same is true for angels. Without variety, they would get bored, too.

Some of the old selfishness from this life may still lurk in their nature and surface occasionally, making life a lot less joyous. But through the process of continually being brought back into the love of God and fellow angels, they are gradually perfected, so that those lapses are less and less likely to occur. And as they pass through each stage of spiritual development, their perception and sense of what is good becomes even more exquisite. The life of heaven only gets better and better, not predictable, routine, and disappointing.

Jesus often compared angels to innocent children, who have complete trust in their parents and no concern about their food, clothing, shelter, or future. They allow themselves to be led.

Angels are in a more adult but similar state of mind. They take no credit for themselves. They don't worry about the necessities of life that so preoccupy us here. They live perfectly content with the leading of the Lord. And while they may appear naive by modern standards, Swedenborg says that the greater the angels' innocence, or willingness to be led, the greater their wisdom and happiness. Those in hell, on the other hand, are totally antagonistic to anything of innocence. And while they may like to think themselves wise, they are utterly ignorant.[30]

Many of us tend to value intelligence more than innocence. Intelligence is what is rewarded most, while innocence is considered out of touch and unsophisticated. But our context is this world, and this world pays more for doing well than being good. A man respected for his intelligence on earth may be quite simple after death if he knows and cares little about spiritual truth. While a man or woman considered simple here but who loves God and tries to live according to His commandments, will be wise in heaven. That wisdom is what is esteemed by the angels.

Swedenborg talked to many people who had been respected for their wisdom in this life. The ones who denied the Divine at heart, no matter how much lip service they gave it, had become so senseless that they could scarcely grasp a civic truth, let alone a spiritual one.[31] But those who had acquired knowledge and applied it to the uses of life, who also loved God and lived a moral life, are those who are meant in the Bible: "They that are intelligent shall shine as with brightness of the firmament, and they shall turn many to righteousness as the stars forever and ever."[32]

The real wisdom of heaven is acknowledgment of God and His truth, and a life that manifests that faith. Angels' lives revolve around that

30. *HH*, pp.277-78, 283.
31. *HH*, p.354.
32. Daniel 12:3.

awareness. But, as the group of angels that had envisioned heaven as constant worship and glorification learned, it does not consume their spiritual life.

There are places of worship in heaven, of course, but worship is much more than an act of prayer. It is made up of each angel's life and all the love, faith, and charity reflected in it. Instruction is given in settings like our churches and synagogues, and worship is focused there. But the real worship comes when that instruction is made a part of life.

Those who love God's teachings and commandments "have in the other life a kind of joyous heavenly warmth."[33] But some people will have nothing to do with such a life. They profane the things of religion and make jokes about it. They "suppose the Word (or Bible) to be of no account except to keep the common people in some restraint."[34] But they are "utterly miserable" in their spiritual life. And the greater their contempt for religion, the greater their misery. The Bible exists in heaven too, in a more clear and spiritual form than what we know. And it is so loved by the angels that anyone who does not share that love cannot be in heaven with them. The sphere of that love would be suffocating to them.[35]

The angels live in societies because "a society is a harmony of many, and no one has life separate from the life of others."[36] Everything in their heavenly environment, even their clothes, reflects their character. You could expect to wear the same sort of clothes you do now, but much finer and more beautiful. Swedenborg says that angels' clothes, like everything else in heaven, are provided in great variety.

"The most intelligent have clothes that gleam as if aflame. The less intelligent have shining white clothes without radiance, and those still less intelligent have clothes of various colors."[37] All of this is determined by the way they understand Divine truth and make it a part of their lives. Those in hell, who have no regard for truth in their lives, wear clothes that are "torn, dirty, and offensive."[38]

Swedenborg likens the language of angels to an indescribable symphony. It is a soft, musical language, and much richer than anything we know. Angels can express in a single word what we would need whole sentences to convey. In this world you may have trouble articulating your feelings, but as an angel you would have none at all. Angels' speech exactly expresses what they are thinking and feeling. There is no groping for the right word.

33. *AC*, p.1,773.
34. *AC*, p.1,878.
35. Ibid.
36. *AC*, p.687.
37. *HH*, p.178.
38. *HH*, p.182.

Heaven is a quite normal but exalted life. These are not angels with wings flitting through clouds. They are real people, living much the same sort of lives as they did on earth, but with absolute bliss and none of the headaches. But what do they do with their time? What can there possibly be for them to do in such a perfect world, where all their needs are taken care of by God?

Obviously many of the things we do in this world aren't needed in heaven. What would a doctor do there, a pilot, an insurance salesman, a mortician? But what we do in this world is for this world. Angelic uses serve very different spiritual needs. Each society in heaven is distinguished by the uses or "goods of charity" it performs. And every angel is happily caught up in doing what he or she really loves. Imagine how heavenly that would be: always to be able to do what you love, for those you love.

Swedenborg says that even though it may be hard to imagine what needs to be done in heaven, there are "so many areas of activity and responsibilities in heaven, so many tasks as well, that they cannot be listed for their abundance. There are few in the world by comparison."[39] It is in this way that the angels express love to each other, and to God.

Some of the obvious things that angels can do for each other are caring for children, teaching and training them as they grow, instructing those newly arrived from earth about the spiritual life and heaven, teaching those who had little religious faith or knowledge in the world but who want to learn, and attending to those being awakened from death to spiritual life.[40] Every angel has a unique responsibility, perfectly suited to his or her temperament. And all of those duties blend into a harmony for the general good.

What you love now and throughout our life on earth will define your rôle in heaven. It may or may not be related to what you do here. Everything in heaven is on a spiritual plane, a dimension we may only glimpse in this world. For instance, plants in heaven have their external beauty but an inner, spiritual quality as well, which represents something of God and elevates the mind of the beholder to Him. A botanist from this earth might "come after death into a knowledge of spiritual uses from the plants of the spiritual world, and cultivate that knowledge with greatest delight."[41]

Those who love their country, its laws and government, and work for its common good, may serve that same love in heaven and its government. Those who are preachers, teachers, administrators, or artists may find similar things to do in heaven, but with a much greater sense of the real service they are performing.

39. *HH*, p.393.
40. *HH*, p.391.
41. *AE*, p.1,211-12.

The uses of heaven are all reciprocal. No one works for honor or gain, because there is no need there for either. The angels work only for the good of each other and for the glory of God. And while they may leave their homes to perform those uses, the home is still the foundation of each angel's life, just as it may be here. And the most reciprocal of all relationships, as well as the highest delight of heaven, is found in each home in the perfect bliss of heavenly marriage.

7

Marriage in Heaven

*I shall but love thee better after
death.*
—Elizabeth Barrett Browning

Those who marry look into each other's eyes and say, "I will love you forever." Then they unite "until death do us part." But where love grows through the years, so does the feeling of forever—that they *will* be together for all time.

Swedenborg assures that the dream is true. Not only do those who truly love each other stay together forever, but their love grows deeper, closer, more devoted and happier than we can possibly imagine.

Even those who haven't found that perfect love on earth, but who have glimpsed it or longed for it, prefer the poet's vision to the theologian's. The dream of love everlasting has been an echoing theme of art and literature, even popular songs. Romeo and Juliet are enduring symbols of lovers consumed by that dream. They die believing they will find a more perfect life and love—and they "shall but love . . . better after death."

But how do we reconcile that hope with what the Bible says, that people in heaven "neither marry nor are given in marriage."[1] Only in what was revealed to Swedenborg can we understand what God meant: not that there is not marriage in heaven, but that it is not the same as it is on earth. Swedenborg shows that marriage in heaven is not only real but is more blissful and perfect than we can ever know on earth. And his writings, especially the volume on *Conjugial Love,* are filled with detail and promise about that ideal love.

He knew that feeling that gives you hope when someone you love dies—that someday you will be together again. "What man who has loved his wife and children," he writes, "does not say within himself when they are dying or have died, that they are in God's hand, and that he will see them again after his own death, and will again be conjoined with them in a life of love and joy."[2]

He gives us a lot more than hope. Not only are men and women still very much men and women after death—not sexless spirits—but every

1. Luke 20:35
2. *CL,* p.28.

angel finds that one perfectly matched partner and the love that really lasts forever. This is love with perfect harmony, total communication of mind and body, and a closeness that brings real oneness. With it comes a sexual relationship more exquisite than anything we can approach on earth. The crowning dimension is a sense of complete unity with God.

Swedenborg exalts the love between a man and a woman as "the universal of all loves . . . implanted by creation in men's very soul, from which is the essence of the whole man."[3] Everything we feel as love stays with us after death, because that is what really makes us who we are. But this love of the opposite sex "especially remains, because any man and woman truly in love yearn for that perfect conjunction of mind and body that will forever bind them together as one."[4]

Whatever your attitude now toward love and marriage, that will stay with you after death, too. Whether it is devoted to one partner, is searching for the ideal, or is lustful and wandering, it isn't going to change miraculously when you die, because that would change who you are. And just as love of the opposite sex in this life often goes from general attraction to a special love for just one, that progression continues after death to a more inward and spiritual love of just one person. And marriage in heaven has a sphere of joy about it that we can scarcely imagine, no matter how happy our marriage on earth may be according to Swedenborg.

We each begin in the other life where we leave off in this one, and the same is true for couples, even though they usually do not die at the same time. When they do meet again they will find that their love for each other, or lack of it, is not changed by death. So when they are reunited, there is the same sense of joy or distance that marked their relationship on earth. The more in love they are, the happier they are to see each other again. But even if there has been something lacking in that love, these reunions are almost always certain to be happy.

In the beginning they are closer to the way they were in this life than in the interior, spiritual life of heaven. This means that their true feelings for each other still may be masked, especially with those who are not genuinely in love. Incompatibility may be hidden under the facade of being nice to each other. But as they come more and more into their interior, true nature, those honest feelings become impossible to conceal. The real quality of their feelings for each other is revealed.

This may sound like it will be a painful, embarrassing experience, but it is much more positive than negative and is essential preparation for heaven. As has been pointed out previously, you cannot hide your true feelings there. And this has to be especially true of marriage in heaven, which is based on complete openness and total conjunction.

3. *CL*, p.46.
4. Ibid.

As couples come to see their love for each other for what it really is, they realize whether or not they can stay together. If their love is mutual, complementary, and devoted, their marriage takes on deeper conviction than they had ever felt on earth and is blessed with a tender joy beyond anything they ever had known.

But if their feelings are discordant, they quickly perceive that theirs is not a marriage for heaven and they separate. That separation may be quite cordial, with full appreciation for what each has given the other and with heartfelt best wishes for each other's happiness. There is the realization that each will be happier with a perfectly suited partner. And most couples want that happiness for each other, even if it cannot be *with* each other. These separations also can be marked with bitterness and quarreling, however, as sore feelings surface.

Whether the separation is pleasant or strained, in circumstances where there must be separation each one in the couple comes to acknowledge that they cannot stay together because there is not enough to bind them. This may be a trying experience, especially where one partner loves more than the other, but it is a merciful process aimed at the ultimate happiness of both. In the gentle, loving sphere of heaven, it is as painless a period as it can be. Separation in heaven from an earthly partner is not easy, particularly where there has been a long and somewhat content relationship, but where it occurs, it does so naturally. It is not forced on anyone but becomes a mutual decision. And it is always for the good of both people and ultimately is turned toward the fulfillment their love longs for.

We may gauge our relationships on this earth on various planes, but in heaven the essential of marriage is the union of two minds, not just two bodies. When a man and woman are perfectly compatible in their minds—in disposition, what they will, and what they love—and when they are in harmony with God as well as each other, then they have true conjugial love. Swedenborg was told by angels that the joy of heavenly marriage grows more and more perfect to eternity and that "the blessings of true marriage love can be listed into many thousands with not even one of them familiar to man."[5]

It is easy to picture those who have enjoyed a really happy marriage on earth continuing in this bliss—forever together, forever happy. But what of others, those unhappily married, those married more than once, those unmarried who wish they were, those who have been promiscuous in place of marriage, and those who have been married but unfaithful to their spouses?

Swedenborg assures that for everyone who enters heaven there is that one conjugial partner, so perfectly complemented that together they

5. *HH*, p.379.

become as one angel. But it may not be an entirely happy journey to that point.

Those who have been married more than once may flounder a bit, going through the entire process from worldly relationships to complete openness of souls with each spouse in turn. They separate from each, as incompatibilities appear, staying with one only if there has been a true conjugial relationship with that one.

Anyone who has abused the marriage relationship may suffer for it during this time, because, from a Swedenborgian viewpoint, anything opposed to marriage is opposed to heaven. The prospects for adulterers—especially those who justify to themselves their infidelity and feel no guilt—are particularly bleak. Swedenborg warns that some of the worst hells are reserved for adulterers.

Those who haven't found a partner but who want to be married will find that perfect mate at last if they go to heaven. Swedenborg does note that some people who have confirmed themselves in a single life may be allowed to enter heaven and remain single. But the real life of heaven is with married partners. Conjugial love is the very sphere of heaven.

How we approach love and marriage in this life actually helps to determine our choice between heaven and hell. Real love leads to heaven and the promise of the greatest happiness we can know. The opposite—adultery and promiscuousness—leads to hell. To the degree that a person chooses adultery to the bonds of marriage, Swedenborg says, he inclines "to the deepest hell, where nothing exists that is not cruel and fearful. This kind of lot awaits adulterers after their life in this world."[6]

If you have not found your partner in this life—the one you want to stay with forever—the obvious question may be, "How will I find that special person in heaven?" Swedenborg describes how couples are led gently by the Lord to find each other. And because they can see everything about the character of each other, they immediately perceive that they are meant for each other and "at first sight they inmostly love each other." There is none of the doubt that may plague the decision in this world, where people often wonder if they know each other well enough. And when they have found each other in heaven, they are married with inspiring ceremony and celebration, and Swedenborg gives a beautiful description of a heavenly wedding he witnessed.[7]

An important part of marriage on this earth is the physical relationship—for its pleasure, for its expression of love, and for procreation. What about heavenly marriage, where the physical and natural plane is superseded by the interior and spiritual and where children are not conceived and born?

6. *HH*, p.386.
7. *CL*, pp.19-22.

Swedenborg assures that the sexual relationship is every bit as important to heavenly marriage, and infinitely more pleasurable. That union in heaven creates a sphere of perfect love with its own "spiritual offspring"—not babies, as here on earth, but new insights into love and wisdom which help the heavenly couple grow together in heavenly love.

There is nothing base or lustful in this sexual relationship, but a potency and pleasure beyond what we can experience on earth. "Those men who are in conjugial love," Swedenborg writes, "are in such a state that they can enjoy intercourse with their wife as often as they please; the ability never fails, inasmuch as all parts of their body are in that love. And, after intercourse, they are affected with joyfulness ... so that they are invigorated by it; but the contrary happens with those who are in adulteries."[8] Swedenborg describes the experience of men, but it is clear from his writing that the pleasure is just as total for women.

Angels told him that,

> they are in continual potency, that after the acts there is never any weariness, still less any sadness, but eagerness of life and cheerfulness of mind, that the married pair pass the night in each other's bosoms as if they were created into one, that they are never lacking when they have desire, since without these their love would be like a channel of a fountain stopped up .... They declare that the delights cannot be described in the expressions of any language in the natural world.[9]

Swedenborg tells of newcomers in the spiritual world laughing among themselves when told by him of the perpetual ability of heavenly partners to enjoy sexual delight, claiming, "What you say is incredible; such ability is not possible. Perhaps you are telling fables."[10]

But an angel suddenly appeared among them, saying that he had lived with his wife for a thousand years "in the same flower of age in which you see me now, and this from living in conjugial love with my wife; and I can assure you that I have had and do now have that perpetual ability."[11]

Such enduring happy relationships are the dream of many who have been in love. And such a love is the promise of heaven for anyone content to love just one partner and to love God. But Swedenborg warns that some who say they want this kind of love may be denying it to themselves by the choices they make in this life. They can deny it by indulging in adultery or things harmful to love. And they can deny it by dominating

8. *SD*, p.6,055.
9. *AE*, p.992.
10. *CL*, p.355.
11. Ibid.

their spouses to the point that there is no love, only a master and servant relationship.

"A love of having one rule over the other" Swedenborg writes, "destroys completely both true marriage love and its heavenly delight."[12] That sense of delight depends on couples working together for each other's happiness, not one taking advantage of the other. It is sharing that brings blessedness to marriage, and dominance that brings detachment between partners.

> Ruling enslaves, and an enslaved mind has either no intention or an opposing one. If there is no intention, there is no love either. If there is an opposing intention, then there is hatred in place of love. The more inward elements of people who live in this kind of marriage clash with each other and struggle like two adversaries, no matter how restrained and composed more outward affairs may be, for the sake of peace and quiet. The clash and struggle of the more inward elements is uncovered after death. They associate a good deal; then they quarrel with each other like enemies.[13]

This does not mean that men and women with unhappy marriages in this life cannot aspire to the happiness of heavenly marriage, and someday find it. This is the real reward for those who may suffer at times in marriages that are less than ideal, but who believe in the sanctity of marriage and work to make the most of their own relationships. But realizing this dream will be harder for those who are used to putting themselves ahead of their partners. The more they do this, the more they also turn themselves away from heavenly marriage. The roles we freely choose to play on earth are the roles we will choose to follow in the other life, because that is how our love guides us.

Even less hope is held out for those who indulge in adultery, because that is the complete opposite of heavenly love. Adulterers shut themselves out of heaven because they never could be happy in its sphere. Adultery poisons marriage and poisons the adulterer. It turns the mind inward to selfishness and away from God and everything that heaven stands for.

Swedenborg notes that "I have been instructed by angels that when anyone commits adultery on earth, heaven is then immediately closed to him" and can only be opened again "by serious repentence."[14] He also tells of those accustomed to seducing others with flattery and guile, who take this ability with them to the spiritual world and "insinuate themselves into societies ... but as their thoughts lie plainly open, they are

---

12. *HH*, p.380.
13. Ibid.
14. *AC*, p.2,750.

everywhere rejected."[15] They are shunned and treated severely because they are out to "steal away the delights and blessedness of others. At length they are admitted into no societies, but after having endured severe punishments are associated with their like in hell."[16] And the hell of the most habitual adulterers, he warns, "is the most grievous of all."[17]

The choice then between heavenly love or the torment of hell is ours to make on earth. Swedenborg consistently holds out the hope that no matter how much we may incline to hell at times, we can always turn to God and heaven. It has to be a serious commitment to mean anything. But with the promise of heaven and a marriage there so full of beauty and happiness, that should be inspiration enough in our lives.

One of the most heartwarming visions in the writings of Swedenborg is of a devoted couple growing old together in this world, then growing young together in heaven, with ever-deepening love. One of the brightest promises there is that such pure and joyous love awaits everyone who truly wants it and lives for it. And one of the saddest scenarios is of the man driven by lust for personal pleasure who finds none in his eternal life, because he has not learned that the essence of love is giving and that the essence of heaven is love.

---

15. *AC*, p.2,753.
16. Ibid.
17. *AC*, p.2,754.

8

Children in Heaven

*Suffer little children to come
unto Me, for of such is the
kingdom of heaven.*
—Matthew 19:14

Headlines announce the daily tragedies:
Three Children Killed in Fire.
Teen Dies in Fiery Crash.
Liver Transplant Baby Dies.

Beyond the headlines are a myriad of private tragedies we never hear about. And beyond every one of them echo the heartbroken questions no one can answer: Why? Why did my baby have to die? Why does God let it happen?

The death of a child is one of the greatest pains to endure. It is a test of faith in a loving, merciful God.

Anyone who knows the tragedy knows doubt and anger as well as grief. But beyond the plaintive, "Why did it happen? Why me?" there comes the wondering, "Where is my child now? Is he in heaven? Is she happy? Is he well cared for? Does she miss me? Will I see him again? Will she remember us?" No one has answers, only hope.

The writings of Swedenborg offer some answers. They explain why, in God's Providence, some children are allowed to die. They describe in such a comforting way what happens to these children, that anyone can find solace, whether a grieving parent or a stranger haunted by a newspaper story.

Swedenborg assures that those who die as children come into their spiritual life at exactly the same stage of development. They are given the most loving, tender care imaginable until they become angels. And, they all do become angels and live forever in heaven, no matter what the circumstances of their birth and life.

We grieve for a life lost before a child has a chance to live. But that child enters into a fullness of life far above what he or she ever would have known on this earth. We rightfully grieve for those left with the heartache of their loss. Nothing will ever replace that child in their lives.

But faith, however hopeful, that the child is happy, well cared for, and thriving in the loving sphere of heaven can begin to counteract grief with comfort.

Swedenborg also assures that however traumatic the death of a child is, especially for those left behind, there is no lingering trauma for the child once death is passed. A child in the spiritual world looks only forward, not back. The future we see as lost to that child is really enhanced. God sees to it that children who come into heaven do not feel sad or lost or fearful without their families and familiar environment, even though they each still have their memory.

They know they will see their families again, and they will rejoice when that time comes. But without the limits of time and space that we are used to, there is no sense of waiting or longing. The child lives only in the present, with no concern for past or future. All the eagerness, enthusiasm, and zest for life is applied to the new life in heaven. And there is plenty in that new life to keep a child busy and content.

That life, no matter how tragic its ending here, opens immediately to a bright and happy world. We are the ones plagued with the questions, "Why? Why this little child? Why me, God?" They are so quickly caught up in the love and happiness of heaven that they feel none of this anxiety.

Swedenborg's writings are filled with insight into why children, as well as adults, come to the end of this life and awaken into their spiritual lives at such various stages of development. Often we say that people have died before their time. But the time is always right in God's Providence. It is right for their development in this life an what they are able to do for others here; and it is right for their spiritual development and what they can do for others in that life.

We may not know what makes it right, of course, so we grieve and question. Only God can see what is best for us in this world *and* in the next. This does not mean that He wants or causes children to die. ("It is not the will of your Father who is in heaven that one of these little ones should perish."[1]) But He does allow things to happen which He does not will, for the sake of our freedom and for the sake of the spiritual potential of each one of us.

He alone knows when it is the right time for a child or adult to leave this world and come into spiritual life, and why. While we may question and doubt in our ignorance, He alone can turn that negative in this world into the ultimate positive in His spiritual kingdom.

Swedenborg notes that the one thing that determines when our time has come is us, meaning what we can do for each other, either through direct action or through the influence of our character. But our usefulness extends beyond our awareness, so that it is hard for us to understand how an "untimely death" could possibly be the right time.

1. Matthew 18:14

Swedenborg wrote in his *Spiritual Diary:*

> Concerning the durations of the life of man, why some live
> long, and some not so long: The life of every man is foreseen
> by the Lord, as to how long he will live, and in what manner;
> wherefore he is directed from earliest infancy with a regard
> to a life of eternity. The Providence of the Lord, therefore,
> commences from earliest infancy. The reason why some die
> as children, some as youths, some as adults, some in old
> age, are:
>
> First, on account of use to man while he is in the world;
>
> Second, on account of use, while he is in the world, to angels
> and spirits (because our internal spheres have influences on
> the spiritual plane, even though we cannot be aware of it);
>
> Third, on account of use to himself in the world, either that
> he may be regenerated, or that he may be let into his evils lest
> they live dormant and afterwards break out, which would
> result in his eternal ruin;
>
> Fourth, on account of use after death and to eternity; for
> everyone who will be in heaven has his place there, or he has
> his place in hell.[2]

None of this may make it any easier to accept the death of a child. But
the idea that there may be a reason, which we may never know but
which is in the best *eternal* interest of the child, eventually may bring
some comfort. Especially with a child who has suffered through illness
or injury or is physically or mentally prevented from living a full life, it
is nice to be able to picture him or her as a normal, happy, and healthy
child growing up in a heavenly environment.

Swedenborg assures that *all* children who die do go to heaven, whether
or not they had been baptized into a faith and no matter how wayward
their parents or their own lives may have been. By "children" Swedenborg
meant all young people under "the age of rationality," which he considers
to be eighteen for women and twenty-one for men. A loving, merciful
God, in His kingdom of perfect justice, is not going to keep a child out
of heaven because of circumstances beyond his or her control.

He notes that "no one gains heaven or faith by means of baptism."
Baptism is an introduction to a faith that provides the means for living
a life for heaven.

> Every infant, wherever he was born—within the church or
> outside it, of godly or of godless parents—every infant is ac-

2. *SD*, p.5,002.

cepted by the Lord when he dies and is brought up in heaven. According to the Divine design, he is taught and filled with affections for what is good. By means of these, he is filled with insights into what is true. Then, as he is made complete in understanding and wisdom, he is introduced into heaven and becomes an angel.

Everyone who thinks rationally is capable of understanding that no one is born for hell, but everyone for heaven; and that the individual himself is at fault for entering heaven, with infants being incapable of fault as yet.[3]

God taught while He was in the world that, "Except ye be converted, and become as little children, ye shall not enter into the kingdom of heaven."[4] And, "Suffer little children to come unto Me, and forbid them not, for of such is the kingdom of God."[5] By this He means that we have to take on the innocence of children—a willingness to be led by God in our lives—in order to become angels. Little children, with their special innocence and trust in others, already have that capacity. Adults, who tend to rely more on themselves, have to work harder at it.

Actually, children who die have something of an advantage, because they still have that innocence that assures them getting into heaven. The evil that can infest our lives and create such a struggle to pressure innocence, is not yet rooted in their lives. They come to heaven readily and naturally. Many adults have to work for it.[6]

Little children come into their spiritual life immediately after death, unlike adults, whose awakening may take as long as three days. They are taken right into heaven and entrusted to the care of angel women "who during their physical life had loved babies tenderly and had also loved God. Because they had in the world loved all babies with a maternal tenderness, they accept these as their own. And the babies, from their inborn nature, love them as though they were their own mothers. Each woman has as many infants as she wants from her spiritual parental affection."[7] These children are led at first into a recognition and belief that the Lord is their own father, and later into a recognition and belief that He is the Lord of everyone and therefore God of heaven and earth.[8]

Children who die come into the spiritual world at exactly the same stage of development they had reached on earth, and with the same diversity of disposition. Their lives are suddenly changed, both dramat-

3. *HH*, p.329.
4. Matthew 18:3.
5. Mark 10:14.
6. *HH*, p.330.
7. *HH*, p.332.
8. *HH*, p.4.

ically and happily. Infants here have to be taught to walk and talk, and their senses, such as sight and hearing, are developed through experience. In their spiritual life, all of this comes naturally and immediately. Swedenborg states that infants who come into heaven "speak the angelic tongue within a month."[9]

They are raised in heaven, but don't become angels until they are grown. That is a process of education and spiritual development. But because it all takes place in the sphere of heaven, each child *will* become an angel. Everything the child learns is from heaven, without any taint from hell. The instruction and development of each child is perfectly adapted to his or her individuality—something we would like to be able to do in this world but rarely can approach. Still, children in heaven are not perfect. They may misbehave or have wayward thoughts and inclinations, but they are gently corrected and they are led to see the error of their ways.

Swedenborg writes that "the Lord flows into infants' concepts . . . for nothing has closed these, as is the case with adults."[10] They are receptive to everything about God and heaven, because there is nothing to cloud their understanding, nothing to keep them from doing good.

Their education is a lot different from what we are used to. There is no need for children in heaven to study much of what they would have to know on this earth—history, geography, languages. They are taught spiritual truth to prepare them for a useful life in heaven, primarily through "representations" especially adapted to their minds.

These are "so beautiful, and so filled from within with wisdom at the same time, that no one could ever believe it. In this way, step by step, an understanding is instilled into them which draws its soul from what is good."[11] These "representatives may include gardens, flowers, trees laden with fruit, gates and arbors, which seem to them to be alive,"[12] just as a child on earth imagines his toys to be alive. "Within such innocent fancies they sense the presence of the Lord."[13]

Each child has his or her own room, bed, clothing, and personal things. Swedenborg notes in his *Spiritual Diary* that they are given coins of gold or silver as rewards for hard work or good behavior, which "they carefully treasure up."[14] They also have their own copies of the written Word—the spiritual rendering of the Bible—which they are encouraged to read and study, either on their own or as part of formal instruction.

Children in heaven are never as trying as they can be on earth, although

9. *SD*, p.5,668.
10. *HH*, p.336.
11. *HH*, p.335.
12.
13. *SD*, p.2, 844.
14. *SD*, p.5,666.

they are still children, who have to learn from mistakes and misbehavior. "When they see spots on their clothes, it is a sign that they have not been thinking well, or have done something wrong. The spots cannot be washed out. When they find out what they have done, they see their blemishes and their evils. If they get the better of them again, the spots disappear.

"When they see that any of their clothes are missing, they immediately know that they have done amiss. They examine themselves, and if they do not know what is wrong, a wife comes who tells them. If they see that there is a new garment in their room, they rejoice, because they know they have done well.

"When they see that the flowers in their little gardens become dim, or change into less attractive ones," they also know that something in their lives is wrong. If the flowers become "better and more beautiful, they rejoice, because it is a sign that they have thought well."[15]

Education is different for children who die at an older age and come into the spiritual world more advanced than infants. Those who have acquired "a good disposition from their education in the world" continue along the same course. "But children who have acquired bad habits of thought, speech, or immoral behavior and been persuaded that there is no evil in such conduct, must be restrained in the World of Spirits under an instructor who may be quite severe with them until they are 'vastated' of the evil.[16]"

All children there grow to young adulthood and remain that "age" forever as angels. At this point, "they are dressed in angelic clothes, most of which are white like linen. They are brought to a path that heads up toward heaven and are committed to angel guardians there; then they are accepted by some other angels and introduced into communities, and there into many forms of happiness."[17]

At this point they also are ready for marriage. And at just the right time the young man and the young woman right for each other "meet somewhere as if by chance. As if by instinct, they instantly know that they are mates; and, as though from a kind of inner dictate, think within themselves, the young man, 'She is mine,' and the maiden, 'He is mine.' After this thought has dwelt for some time in the minds of both, they deliberately address each other and are betrothed."[18] Soon after they are married and enter together into the joys of heavenly marriage and heaven itself.

Any parent who has lost a child should be comforted by this vision. On the other hand, Swedenborg warns that parents can turn their children against heaven by inciting the wrong behavior in this life.

15. *SD*, pp.5, 664-56.
16. *SW*, p.154.
17. *HH*, p.519.
18. *CL, p.316.*

I was in the street of a great city and saw little boys fighting with one another. A crowd gathered and looked on with much pleasure, and I was informed that the parents themselves urge on their little boys in such fights. The good spirits and angels who saw these things through my eyes were so averse to them that I perceived their horror, especially at the fact that the parents incite them to such things, saying that thus in their earliest age they extinguish all the mutual love and all the innocence which little children receive from the Lord, and initiate them into hatred and revenge; consequently that they deliberately shut out their children from heaven, where there is nothing but mutual love. Let parents who wish well to their children beware of such things.[19]

Even this extreme does not keep a child out of heaven. It just makes heaven more remote. Once in heaven, a child has everything from God on his or her side. So out of the tragedy of an infant, child, or young person taken "before his time," we gain comfort from seeing what happens to that loved one taken from us. Faith will not completely take away the pain of loss, but what we see here is perfect love and care in heaven, ideal education, absolute happiness, and finally the perfect marriage and the perfect bliss of heaven.

19. Ibid.

9

If I Make My Bed in Hell

*The hell to be endured
hereafter is no worse than the
hell we make for ourselves in
this world by habitually
fashioning our characters in
the wrong way.*
—William James

Hell is not some foreign, faraway place. We don't have to wonder what it's like. We've been there.

Just as heaven can be around us and within us, so can hell. We see it in crime and brutality, greed and dishonesty. We feel it when we are filled with unjust anger and ill will, lust, or selfishness.

No one is immune from the influence of hell. We can't keep it out of our minds. We *can* try to keep it out of our lives. It is feeling the presence of both heaven and hell in our lives that gives us the freedom to make the choice.

You might be wondering, Who would ever choose hell? Probably no one would admit to "choosing" hell. But people do choose to live lives opposed to heaven, and they will find the only home for that life in hell.

Most of us aren't proud of the ugly moments in our lives when we let hell in. We feel shame, regret, and determination to be more patient, less selfish—whatever it takes. The more repentant we feel, and the more we try to keep that ugliness out of our lives, the closer we are to heaven. The more that anger, hate, selfishness, and deceit become a way of life, with satisfaction in place of remorse, the more the choice is made to "make my bed in hell."

Whatever concept we have of hell, whether the burning pits of myth or just some vague world of horror, it's enough to scare us, because we know we have something of hell in us—its selfishness, its hatred, its deceit. Even the most upright people can feel hellish inside sometimes, with thoughts and fantasies no one must ever know about. That leaves all of us not feeling good about ourselves at times. But the Bible teaches, and Swedenborg confirms, that we are not responsible for what comes into our minds, only for what we choose to make a part of our lives.

That choosing is a lifelong process and can be a lifelong struggle. Part of choosing heaven, for instance, is turning aside those darker thoughts and instincts, whether they take the form of lust or revenge, arrogance or selfishness. That is easy to resolve in moments of self-evaluation, harder to do when temptation strikes. But giving in to those ugly urges—from cutting off someone in traffic, to lying or coveting—makes hell a conscious part of life. It may last only a moment, or if it becomes a pattern, forever.

If you are afraid of going to hell because of things you have done or thought that you know aren't heavenly—and who doesn't have that fear at times—bear in mind that you only will go to hell if that is where you choose to go. Swedenborg assures that no one is going to make you go to hell. No one is going to send you there as punishment for a wicked life. No one is going to condemn you there against your will. People go to hell only because that is where they really want to be. They want to be there because that is where the life is that they have chosen for themselves. It's home.

Hell is home for liars, thieves, murderers, adulterers, cheats—people who stop at nothing to hurt others and satisfy themselves. No wonder Swedenborg says that people from hell who are allowed into heaven want to get away as fast as they can. And no wonder that the angels find everything about hell repulsive.

Hell is as close or as far away from us as we want it to be. It is easy to get so wrapped up in day-to-day living that many of us seldom stop to reflect on the choices that are shaping our destiny. But while God never stops trying to raise us up to heaven, the hells never stop trying to drag us down.

We help them out and bring hell close when we do what we know is wrong—cheating, lying, hurting someone—especially if we enjoy it or feel no conscience about it. It may be a fleeting mood, when we are upset or angry, or it may be a lingering cloud. But it is something we *can* bring upon ourselves, and it is comething we also *can* put out of our lives, if we really work at it. In his *Paradise Lost* John Milton rightly says, "The mind is its own place, and in itself can make a heaven of hell, a hell of heaven."[1]

Swedenborg agrees that people who go to hell start on the way by making their own hells in this life, and they do it primarily through lives that focus on themselves. Think of how opposite that is to heaven, where life revolves around loving God and doing things for others. In heaven, love flows out. In hell, it spirals inward and is self-consuming.

1. Milton, *Paradise Lost*, bk. 1, l.253.

We may like to think that hell is only for really evil people, the kind of evil we associate with murder, rape, sadism, atrocity. But Swedenborg defines the evil of hell as simply a love of self that turns away from God. That is a lot more pervasive.

We have an idea of heaven as "up there" and hell "down below," and that is how Swedenborg describes the appearance in the World of Spirits. The entrances to heaven wind upward while "there are hells everywhere—under the mountains, the hills, the cliffs, under the plains and valleys. The opening of the gates to the hells . . . look like crevices or clefts in the rocks. Some spread broad and ample, some are tight and narrow; most are jagged. All of them look dark and gloomy . . . (with) the kind of light which burning torches give."[2] The eyes of hells' inhabitants are adapted to this light so that it seems bright enough to them. But it is nothing like the dazzling brightness of heaven, which they could never tolerate.

These hells are as numerous as the heavens. Part of the order of heaven and hell is that there is an opposite hell for every society in heaven.[3] And just as there are three levels of heaven, distinguished by the spiritual quality of the angels, there are three levels of hell, ranging from mild to severe.

"In some hells," Swedenborg writes, "one can see something like the rubble of homes and cities after a great fire, where hellish spirits live and hide. In milder hells one sees something like tumble-down huts, crowded together rather like a city, with sections and streets. Within the houses are hellish spirits, so there are constant brawls, hostilities, beatings and clawings. There are robberies and holdups in the streets."[4] (Remember, this is to the eyes of someone not living in hell. To those who live there it is a perfectly normal world, a world that symbolizes everything they love.)

Another vivid description, culled from the writings of Swedenborg, is offered by Dr. Hugo Odhner:

> This underworld would be seen as a place of oppressive heat or of extreme cold, of darkness and confusing horrors, a world gone to ruin by neglect and misuse. The dwellings are miserable caverns, tumbling shanties, or half-wrecked cities, steeped in filth and encroached upon by poisonous jungles and marshes, full of decaying vegetation and ferocious beasts, pestiferous insects, bogs and quicksands, and rocky deserts, angry seas and treacherous whirlpools, and regions

2. *HH*, p.584.
3. *HH*, p.588, 541.
4. *HH*, p.586.

subject to flood and volcanic eruptions. The soil itself is often septic, barren and foul, and the air is heavy with evil stenches.[5]

Quite a contrast to heaven, isn't it?

> He continues: But the most incredible truth is that all this is what evil spirits love! Create for them a clean and fruitful paradise, and they would soon transform it into a filthy and ugly wilderness, in which alone they would feel at home. It seems impossible to imagine that they could enjoy the discomforts, deprivations, and sufferings which such wretched surroundings bring about. Yet we must remember that an infernal spirit loves his own evils, and a part of his environment is the projection of his own states of mind. It is the mental world in which he glories, and it contains all the evils which he has justified as good and delightful and thinks of as desirable because they give him a sense of power and self-importance.[6]

"Hellfire" is one of the myths we associate with hell, but Swedenborg explains that it is more appearance than fact. People in hell don't live amid licking flames, as artists and cartoonists would have us believe. There is a sphere of fire and heat around them, though, which represents their burning anger and lusts.[7]

Another common assumption about hell is that it is ruled by one devil, or Satan. Swedenborg notes that references to Satan, the devil, and Lucifer in the Bible are representative. There is no one supreme devil who was a rebellious angel who now rules hell. One reason is that hell has its origin in our own minds. Everyone in hell once lived on earth. Taken together they all represent the devil.[8]

If they were in control, the hells would be much worse than they are. The very first teaching given in the writings of Swedenborg about hell is that God alone rules there, as well as in heaven, because only He can keep it under control. That confirms what the Psalmist says: "If I ascend up into heaven, Thou art there: if I make my bed in hell, behold, Thou art there."[9]

The reason for this is the equilibrium between heaven and hell, which preserves our freedom to choose either. Unless God ruled both worlds,

5. Dr. Hugo Odhner, *The Spiritual World* (Bryn Athyn, Pa.: Academy Publications Committee, 1968), p.321.
6. Ibid., p.322.
7. *HH,* p.570.
8. *HH,* p.544.
9. Psalm 139:8.

this equilibrium could not exist. Then there would be real danger that the pressures from hell could become so great, overwhelming inclinations to evil already in us, that we would lose our ability to resist, and our freedom to choose.[10]

Swedenborg says that angels are allowed to restrain and moderate what goes on in hell. "But in a broad sense, all the people who are in the hells are governed by their fears,"[11]—primarily the fear of punishment.

> There are many kinds of punishment, milder or more severe depending on their evil deeds. For the most part, the more vicious ones are given authority over the others. They hold sway by means of their cunning and their skills, and are able to keep the rest in compliance and slavery by means of punishments and the resulting dread. These authorities dare not go beyond limits set for them. It is worth knowing that the fear of penalties is the only means of controlling the ferocity and rages of the people in the hells. No other means exist.[12]

Punishment does not mean that they are physically punished forever for sins committed in this life. Hell itself is the fulfillment of a life given over to evil. But punishment and the fear of it are used to keep control over what they would do to each other if they were free to do as they wanted.

It's a two-way process. Everyone in hell is subject to punishment—which takes the form of mental torment and anguish rather than physical abuse—but loves to inflict punishment as well. They would rather hurt than help those around them, and make them miserable instead of happy. "The greatest delight in their life consists in being able to punish, torture, and torment one another, and this by arts unknown in the world, whereby they know how to induce exquisite suffering, and dreadful and horrid fantasies."[13]

They have almost hypnotic powers over each other, and can induce mental tortures more vivid than nightmares and like the terrifying hallucinations of mental illness.

The angels of heaven help to maintain order, but, some inhabitants of hell are allowed to have some control over others. The love of dominating others is called "the most virulent lust of hell."[14] The most evil and domineering gain control over others and control them by fear. They hate anyone who doesn't fawn over them. But as with all despots, their

10. *HH*, pp. 536, 540.
11. *HH*. p. 543.
12. Ibid.
13. *AC*, p.695.
14. Odhner, p.343.

control is insecure and precarious, because their unwilling subjects are constantly recruiting allies and plotting rebellion. Meanwhile, those in power may band together and help each other when there is a common enemy, but once the threat passes, they turn against each other. We see it happens in this world all the time. It is only more blatant in hell.[15]

The Golden Rule that we know from the Bible ("Do unto others as you would have them do unto you") is the way of life in heaven. Hell has its own version, which amounts to, "You leave me alone and I'll leave you alone." But the inhabitants are always maneuvering for advantage, so that retaliation is more the rule than cooperation. They live to instill fear, not goodwill. They live only for themselves, not for others. There is no sense of community with them, no common purpose to unite them, no growth. There is nothing of the peace and goodwill of heaven. In hell there is only tension, turmoil, and suspicion.

Who would ever choose such a life? Well, people are choosing it all the time by living it: living with lies, deceit, cruelty, selfishness. And because they have made this their life, because they have rejected God and heaven in their lives, they seek out hell when they get that opportunity. They have, in fact, already chosen it before they get there.

Those who choose hell, however, don't go there until their hellish nature is exposed and any sham of a good life put on for others is removed. In this world they may have tried to appear good, to help their own ends. Now they feel no self-consciousness about expressing their true feelings. There is no embarrassment about who and what they are, no shame and no regret.[16]

When they come into hell, they are "received warmly at first and believe they have arrived among friends. However, this lasts for only a few hours."[17] Evil spirits explore their character for weaknesses to exploit and infest them with their evil nature "until they are reduced to slavery."[18]

It is a never-ending process. "Since revolutionary movements are constantly arising there (for everyone there wants to be greatest, and is on fire with hatred for the others), there are new uprisings. So one situation gives way to another. This means that the enslaved members are freed to lend their strength to some particular new devil in order to conquer others. Then the people who do not give in and obey the leader's whim are again tormented in different ways. This goes on and on."[19]

Angels are described as incredibly beautiful because their faces and bodies reflect their love. So do the features of those in hell manifest their nature. They may look lustily attractive to each other, but in the light of

15. Ibid.
16. Odhner, p.340.
17. *HH*, p.574.
18. Ibid.
19. Ibid.

heaven their faces are described by Swedenborg as "frightful, lifeless as corpses. Some are black, some like fiery little torches, some swollen by pimples, distorted veins and sores. Many have no visible face, but only something hairy or bony instead. Their bodies are bestial and their speech apparently arises from anger or hatred or revenge . . . . All of them are reflections of their own hells."[20]

They aren't loathsome to one another, of course, because they are all kindred spirits and love what they see in themselves and each other. Only when light comes in from heaven do they see themselves for what they are. "This is why they run away from heaven's light and plunge into their own light."[21]

The life of hell, to anyone not in its sphere, is as repulsive as its inhabitants. All the ill will held back in this life breaks out in the open in hell. It is a life filled with bitterness, discontent, deception, cruelty, and failure, a world of mental torture and frustration. Imagine how you feel when nothing works out right, when you can't finish what you set out to do, when what you really want is thwarted. That is a taste of hell.

In Swedenborg's revelation everything about heaven is represented in the unity of perfect heavenly marriage. There is no unity in hell, in thought or among people. Instead of couples living for each other, as in heaven, there are individuals living only for themselves. There is no marriage in hell; there are not even permanent partners.
Dr. Odhner writes that

> . . . spiritual adulteries find their expressionin all manner of illicit relations, so that the hells display all kinds of sexual perversions, many of which are described in Swedenborg's diary.
>
> There is neither mutual love nor any mutual respect between the sexes, but a contemptuous rivalry by which each seeks to dominate the other by compulsion or subtle cunning. Their sex life is sordid, and by degrees its fever is turned into coldness, hate and aversion, into rejection, blasphemy, contention and open fights. For adulterous love is fiery in externals, but cold in internals, and ends in frustration, impotence, and unhappiness.[22]

In spite of all this, Swedenborg was repeatedly told by those in hell that "they would a thousand times rather live in hell than out of it.

20. *HH*, p.553.
21. Ibid.
22. Odhner, pp.330-31.

Nowhere else can they indulge in their sole delight, which is to see others suffer and thus boost their own sense of importance. Nowhere but in hell can they escape contact with the sphere of conjugial love, innocence and charity from heaven, which causes them nausea and aversion."[23]

One thing that spirits cannot escape, in hell or in heaven, is work. The difference is that in heaven the angels welcome the opportunity and are blissfully content, doing what they love to do. In hell, all work is drudgery, and there is no getting away from it. It is like a slave labor camp, where everyone is forced to work for his good. No one is allowed to be idle or useless. But they get no pleasure from the work they have to do. It is only the fear of punishment or not getting what they want that keeps them at it.

The work that they do is in an environment of squalor and filth, but that is what suits them because it represents what they love. Swedenborg describes the hells of those who love robbery, lying, adultery, pleasure and greed, and recalls a robber who "confessed that he would rather live in urinous filth than by the clearest waters."[24]

The hells for adulterers were said to be increasing, even in Swedenborg's time, and to be particularly repulsive. The harshest punishments are for men who delight in seducing and prostituting virgins. Those who love vulgarity take that crudeness with them and are humiliated for it in the spiritual world. Women who enjoy seducing men and manipulating them to their advantage also incline toward the lower hells, "seeming to live among snakes."[25]

People so caught up in looking out for themselves and climbing over others to get ahead are likely to think the least about life after death, Swedenborg says. And when they come into that life they seem to themselves "to be busy in cellars where their money is, and to be infested there by mice."[26]

Those who have given themselves over to pleasure and ease, with no regard for God, heaven, or their neighbor, find a life in stark contrast to the pampered existence they had worshiped. But Swedenborg is careful to point out that wealth and "the good life" do not doom anyone to hell. It is only those who come to value worldliness and selfishness over caring for others who doom themselves.[27]

He also offers hope for all of us who worry about the dark side of our nature—the thoughts and fantasies we would be ashamed to have others see. He assures that we are not held accountable for the heredity with which we are born, or the wayward tendencies that come with it, unless we choose to make them our own.

23. Ibid., p.331.
24. AC, p.820.
25. AC, pp.824-30.
26. AC, p.938.
27. AC, p.943-5.

Conscience is what helps us to rise above the vagrant inclinations that plague our lives and allows us to approach heaven. Those who choose to live without heaven in their lives also live without conscience and set their course for hell. While God continually forgives our transgressions, forgiveness does not take away those baser inclinations. It is giving their lives over to them that turns people, by their own choice, away from heaven and toward hell.

The picture Swedenborg paints of hell is close to what we see on earth with those whose lives are ruled by lust, selfishness, and ill will. Their pleasure comes at the expense of someone else's happiness. But it's a pleasure warped by fear of retaliation and discovery.

The fear of hell may encourage a determination to do better with our lives, but what is done solely out of fear isn't enough. It is useful to know what hell is really like so that we can know what to fear and what to shun, but it will only be meaningful if it becomes "holy fear." That is a fear that springs from love. It is absolute aversion to doing anything that would hurt God or anyone. The fear of letting down others translates into the love that works for their happiness. This is ultimately what saves us from hell, not just the fear of it.

The writings of Swedenborg expose in stark and terrifying terms the hidden hells that lurk in the dark corners of our minds. But they also show the way to close those doors forever and open the way to heaven.

10

Coming Home

*One thing have I desired of the
Lord, that will I seek after; that
I may dwell in the house of the
Lord all the days of my life.*
—*Psalm 27:4*

Why was Swedenborg permitted to describe heaven and hell in such detail? It was not just to serve our curiosity, but to add meaning and purpose to our lives.

The meaning of life is a mystery as old as life itself. Eternal life is the answer.

How much we know about eternal life has a lot to do with how much we believe in it. And how much we believe in it has a lot to do with the meaning in our lives, or lack of it.

A sure faith in life after death adds meaning to marriage, to work, to death, and many of the things in life we cannot understand. Without that faith we may grope for meaning.

Swedenborg's mission was to make heaven and hell real to us. We are able to see them not only as real after death, but as a real part of this life. We feel the influence of each and make our choice for one or the other through our lives. The meaning of life is the kind of choice we make of life.

Having an idea of what we may expect helps us to prepare for life after death and adds perspective for measuring life here. We can stop and look at the choices, the patterns and the spiritual potential of our lives and ask if we are satisfied with what we see. If not, we can focus on what we need to change and go to work on it.

Swedenborg says at the end of *Heaven and Hell,* "What we have presented in this book about heaven, the world of spirits, and hell will be obscure to people who find no delight in knowing spiritual truths; but they will be clear to people who do find this delight. This is particularly true for people involved in an affection for what is true for its own sake . . . Anything that is loved brings light with it into the mind's concepts."[1]

1. *HH,* p.603.

Part of the problem with developing faith in life after death is that we aren't inclined to think about death until we have to. And we usually don't live with much of a sense that our lives on earth are shaping our lives after death.

Some people live with an active faith in life after death. For others there is more hope than faith. For still others there is more doubt and wondering than hope or faith. There are plenty of people just trying to live a good life for its own sake, without the motivation of a "reward" in heaven. There are others who believe in reincarnation, or nothing at all after death. For some people life after death is just too fanciful a concept to accept without proof. Others may want to believe but lack conviction. Some are satisfied that a life after death and heaven and hell just has to be, because somewhere there must be justice. But for many of us, whether or not there is a life after death is not an active concern in our day-to-day lives.

The events of this world naturally dominate our lives. We have to cope with the various pressures and relationships of this life, and the affairs of the world clamor for our attention. Our spiritual life is more abstract, not as clearly defined, but affects everything we do. That is the life that is going to last forever. That is the life that needs attention and preparation.

There is no more significant change in life than death, but what have you done to prepare for it, and for the life to follow? If you don't know what to plan for or how to prepare yourself, that isn't easy. The teachings given through Swedenborg let us know what we may expect and how to prepare.

Basically they teach that the life that leads to heaven is a spiritual life. That doesn't mean a pious life is an important part of spiritual life, but what really counts is what you do with what you believe.

We have seen how those who expected heaven to be little more than exalted worship were allowed to experience that and felt suffocated by it. They learned what we all need to learn: that the life of heaven, and the life that leads to it, is one of cheerful usefulness, not isolation. It is centered in God and focused on the neighbor, not self.

Genuinely happy people in this world are not those who measure happiness in wealth, possessions, and getting their way. They are those spiritually at peace with God and themselves. That is the beginning of real heavenly happiness. Some of the things we strive for—wealth, reputation, and influence—can be blessings if they contribute to our usefulness. But they can be curses if they become ends in themselves, leaving people feeling miserable and unfulfilled in spite of their power and possessions. Happiness and contentment belong to spiritual life.

The constant message of the Bible is to put the life of heaven before the life of this world. The promise is that this will make life in this world happier and more fulfilling.

The Sermon on the Mount advises, "Lay not up for yourselves treasures upon earth, where moth and rust doth corrupt, and where thieves break through and steal. But lay up for yourselves treasures in heaven, where neither moth nor rust doth corrupt, and where thieves do not break through nor steal. For where your treasure is, there will your heart be also."[2]

And, "For your heavenly Father knoweth that ye have need of all these things. But seek ye *first* the kingdom of God and His justice, and all these things shall be added unto you."[3]

There is also the familiar teaching, "For what is a man profited if he shall gain the whole world and lose his own soul?"[4]

Swedenborg adds, "Let him who wishes to be eternally happy know and believe that he will live after death. Let him think of this and keep it in his mind, for it is true. Let him also know and believe that the Word (Bible) is the only doctrine that teaches how a man must live in the world in order to be happy to eternity."[5]

He also warns that the more we are preoccupied with this world, the less receptive we are to hearing and thinking about our eternal life to come. "Such spirits abound in the world of spirits and prompt man to indulge his natural inclinations and to live for himself alone and those who favor him. In order for man to be uplifted he must think about eternal life."[6]

That isn't always easy. We struggle to find meaning in life, but struggle all the more if we narrow our focus to this world instead of enlarging it to spiritual life. That is where real meaning lies. The reason why these teachings were given is to adds perspective for thinking spiritually about life and where it is taking us. Swedenborg says our belief in life after death or denial of it inmostly qualifies all our thinking and ultimately determines our values.

There are many teachings in the Bible about heaven, but they may leave us hungering for more. The teachings given through Swedenborg build on the biblical promise. They are clear, direct, and beautifully detailed. They also show that putting heaven first in life does not exclude a useful, happy, and stimulating existence in this world. It makes it all the more likely that your life in the world will be productive, fulfilling, peaceful, and happy.

The search for heaven begins with the search for meaning in life. Some people fluctuate between confidence and doubt about who they are and what their life means. Others are certain only of their uncertainty and wonder, Who am I? Why am I here? What does it mean?

2. Matthew 6:19-21.
3. Matthew 6:32-33.
4. Matthew 16:26.
5. *AC*, p.8,939.
6. *AC*, p.6,201.

For those who do not have in mind that God's goal for us in heaven, the search can be a treadmill of frustration. For those who believe, as Swedenborg emphatically teaches, that everyone is created for heaven and everyone who wants it can be there, the meaning of life is clear.

Dr. Odhner writes, "The object of life, here as well as hereafter, is to break the walls that hinder us from understanding each other; to escape from the shadows of pride and envy and misconception; and to let the light of truth shine into our souls so that we can recognize ourselves and our place and use in the commonwealth of spiritual life."[7]

The trouble is, we may keep setting our course for heaven but find ourselves distracted. God's constant leading to heaven is likened by Swedenborg to a stream. It never stops and its destination never changes. Like twigs tossed by waves and currents, we can slip the stream and get caught up in whirlpools and eddies. We feel the pull both ways. We can go with God's current or make our own way.

The lure of hell to selfish pleasure can be more tempting at times than the quiet, spiritual allures of heaven. Traditional morality is countered with a new ethic: If it feels good, do it. And if everyone's doing it, it can't be bad. But on these rocks many a promising life may be dashed.

The questions to keep asking yourself are, On the basis of my life so far, how am I projecting eternity? Is what I see what I want? What am I becoming? Am I becoming more angelic through my life, or less so? And what can I do to change?

Everyone has inclinations to hell. You know that from the dark side of your nature. But you know you have a yearning for heaven's peace as well. To be aware of your baser instincts and want to improve is the first step to heaven. Not to care and to justify and indulge those base instincts is the first step to hell. Throughout your life, you know both heaven and hell. More and more you set a path to one or the other, by your free choice.

While you are setting that spiritual path, you are much more likely to have your eyes on where you are going in this life. So much of what we call success in life is measured in worldly terms. Death is the great equalizer. When you arrive in the spiritual world, it isn't going to matter how much money you made, how many honors pad your resume, how famous you were. All that matters is what kind of a person you are.

It isn't going to make any difference to anyone there if you were a lawyer, doctor, politician, author, movie star, or athlete. Here that sort of thing may command respect and confer superiority. People of simple life and accomplishment on earth may be "richer" in heaven than those who had lorded their wealth over them. ("But many that are first shall be last; and the last shall be first."[8])

7. Odhner, p.200.
8. Matthew 19:30.

Mark Twain wrote on his death bed, with considerable insight, "Death, the only immortal who treats us all alike, whose pity and whose peace and whose refuge are for all—the soiled and the pure, the rich and the poor, the loved and the unloved."[9]

Through the ages there has been plenty of insight and speculation about death, confidence and wondering, fear and hope.

Leonardo da Vinci certainly had no fear. He said, "As a well-spent day brings happy sleep, so life well-used brings happy death."[10]

John Donne wrote confidently in his *Holy Sonnets* in 1635: "One short sleep past, we wake eternally, And death shall be no more: death, thou shalt die."[11] Longfellow found an apt analogy in the famous covered bridge in Lucerne: "The grave itself is but a covered bridge, leading from light to light, through a brief darkness."[12]

> Back in the 1600s an Englishman named Thomas Fuller proclaimed, "No man who is fit to live need fear to die." To us here, death is the most terrible thing we know. But when we have tasted its reality it will mean to us birth, deliverance, a new creation of ourselves. It will be what health is to the sick man; what home is to the exile; what the loved one given back is to the bereaved. As we draw near to it a solemn gladness should fill our hearts. It is God's great morning lighting up the sky. Our fears are the terrors of children in the night. The night with its terrors, its darkness, its feverish dreams, is passing away; and when we awake it will be into the sunlight of God.[13]

Two centuries later, a Scottish clergyman named Norman McLeod offered this thought: "We picture death as coming to destroy; let us rather picture God as coming to save. We think of death as ending; let us rather think of life as beginning, and that more abundantly. We think of losing; let us think of gaining. We think of going away; let us think of arriving. And as the voice of death whispers, 'You must go from earth,' let us hear the voice of God saying, 'You are but coming to me.'"[14]

We fear death because of the unknown, and because of foreboding

9. Mark Twain, *The Autobiography of Mark Twain*, (New York: Harper, 1953).

10. Leonardo Da Vinci, *Notebooks*, trans. by Edward McCurdy (New York: Modern Library, 1957).

11. John Donne, *Poetical Works* (London: Oxford University Press, 1973).

12. Henry Wadsworth Longfellow, *The Poems of Henry Wadsworth Longfellow* (New York: Heritage Press, 1943).

13. *Notable Men and Sayings of England* (London: International Library of Famous Literature, 1874).

14. Ibid.

about being judged. Swedenborg makes clear that the ultimate judgment of whether you go to heaven or hell is self-judgment. No one is going to make you go where you don't want to go.

Sometimes fear of life seeks escape in embracing death through suicide. Swedenborg warns that it is no escape, that such people, when they come into the spiritual world, have to endure the same frenzy, anxiety, despair or whatever pushed them to it, until they have finally worked their way through their problems.

Medical scientists are trying to find ways to postpone death by extending life, from real advances in organ transplants to more exotic theories of freezing bodies until cures or organs become available. It sometimes seems almost a desperate attempt to avoid confronting life after death and the judgment that holds us accountable for our life on earth. How much happier it is, for many, to live with the faith that the life after death can be immeasurably better than any life we can know on earth, to live for the richness of that life and look forward to it.

Those who have a negative, fearful view of death have a torment in their lives almost totally lacking in those who have a peaceful, confident faith and hope for heaven. One positive view you can have of death is that it frees you to fulfill your destiny. You may begin to live in heaven through your life on earth, but cannot enter into it fully until you leave this life. As Michelangelo put it: "Death and love are the two wings that bear the good man to heaven."[15]

It would be nice to have a sure sense of where you are going, amid the hectic distractions of this world. But think of migratory birds flying through storms and across great expanses of water and unknown country. How do they know where they are going? How do we, unless we put our trust in God to guide us?

Robert Browning put it this way in his poem "Paracelsus":

I go to prove my soul!
I see my way as birds their trackless way.
I shall arrive! What time, what circuit first,
I ask not; but unless God send His hail
Or blinding fireballs, sleet or stifling snow,
In some time, His good time, I shall arrive:
He guides me and the bird. In His good time![16]

People who have faith and try to live according to it seem to have more peace of mind and a surer sense of where they are going than those who

15. Howard Hibbard, *Michelangelo* (New York:Harper & Row, 1974).
16. Robert Browning, *The Complete Poetical Works of Robert Browning* (New York: Macmillan, 1915).

look to the world and find a confusion of signals. But for all of us, life is like the experience of Moses and the Children of Israel wandering the wilderness for forty years, seeking the Promised Land. Heaven is that Promised Land, and God constantly is leading us to it. He led the Israelites the same way. Sometimes they doubted and wanted to go their own way, just as we do. But His leading never stopped. So it is with each of us in the wilderness of life. It is tuning in to that leading that makes the difference in people's lives.

Swedenborg emphasizes time and again that every one of us can be delivered, out of the wilderness into the Promised Land, no matter what our circumstances. He steadfastly assures that God leaves no one without the means to be saved, no matter how ignorant, deprived, evil, or undeserving he or she may appear to be. In fact, everyone is said to be "born for heaven." That is what God wills for every one of us. It is only our own free choice that can take any one of us to hell instead.

Swedenborg also assures that heaven is open to everyone, including those raised without baptism or instruction in a formal faith. Those "who have led a moral life, living in obedience and good order and mutual charity according to their religious persuasion, and who have thereby acquired some element of conscience, they have been accepted in the other life and are taught there with painstaking care by angels, about the good and true elements of faith. I have been told that when they are taught, they behave temperately, understandingly, and wisely, readily accepting truths and absorbing them."[17]

He also assures that heaven is not as remote as we might imagine. Some people believe that the life that leads to heaven is difficult, because they have been told they have to renounce the world, get rid of "lusts of body and flesh," and live a life of piety. But Swedenborg says this is not true.

"People who renounce the world and live by the spirit in this fashion build up a mournful life for themselves, one that is not receptive of heavenly joy; for everyone's life awaits him. On the contrary, if a person is to accept heaven's life, he must live in the world, involved in its functions and deadlines. Then through a moral and civic life he receives a spiritual life. This is the only way a spiritual life can be formed in a person, or his spirit prepared for heaven."[18]

The idea is not to withdraw from the world but to live a life *in* the world that reflects the life of heaven: honesty, justice, goodwill, and delight in going things for others. It is not piety and self-examination alone which are important, but also an active life that looks outward.

The teachings given through Swedenborg are the most extensive and

17. *HH*, p.321.
18. *HH*, p.528.

most detailed we have about heaven and hell and the life that leads to each. They can help you cope with your own life and death, as well as the death of those close to you. By making heaven real and attainable, they can change your life, forever.

They also encourage confidence that death is a natural part of life and a beginning, not an end. There may still be apprehension when transition comes. But the more real life after death is to you, the more the grave becomes a doorway to a great adventure, not something closed and cold and final which you dread. That is the faith that gives purpose to death and meaning to life.

RECOMMENDED SWEDENBORG FOUNDATION PUBLICATIONS AND FILMS ON RELATED SUBJECTS

Books about Swedenborg:

THE SWEDENBORG EPIC: The Life and Works of Emanuel Swedenborg
By Cyriel Odhner Sigstedt (Swedenborg Society, London)
The classic biography of Swedenborg.

THE ESSENTIAL SWEDENBORG
By Sig Synnestvedt
A presentation of the basic elements of Swedenborg's thought.

THE PRESENCE OF OTHER WORLDS: The Psychological/Spiritual Findings of Emanuel Swedenborg
By Wilson Van Dusen
A clinical psychologist's account of Swedenborg's inward journey, which resulted in strikingly modern writings about the psyche.

MY RELIGION
By Hellen Keller
Helen Keller's inspiring personal account of Swedenborg's writings as a source of her own courage and strength.

THE HOLY CENTER
By Dorothea Harvey
A presentation of elements of Jewish ritual with ecumenical breadth and personal insight, as symbolic of contemporary spiritual values and processes.

Books by Emanuel Swedenborg

HEAVEN AND HELL

Swedenborg's revolutionary vision of the afterlife as an extension of the inner realities of the psyche.

ARCANA COELESTIA (HEAVENLY SECRETS) 12 volumes
A detailed analysis of the symbolic meanings of the books of Genesis and Exodus as guides to the unfoldment of human consciousness.

THE APOCALYPSE REVEALED 2 volumes
A similar analysis of the subtext of the enigmatic Book of Revelation, with particular emphasis on inner changes in the Christian church.

THE APOCALYPSE EXPLAINED 6 volumes
A comprehensive examination of most of the Book of Revelation, with copious references to other books of the Bible.

DIVINE LOVE AND WISDOM
A far-reaching philosophical/religious exploration of love as the basis of existence.

DIVINE PROVIDENCE
A sequel to the above, celebrating free will as an inherent principle of the divine master plan.

TRUE CHRISTIAN RELIGION
Swedenborg's own systematization of his theological writings into a unified vision of a new age with beliefs predicated on inner realities rather than outward forms.

JOURNAL OF DREAMS
With commentary by Wilson Van Dusen
Only recently available in English, Swedenborg's private dream journal reveals an eighteenth century scientist struggling to interpret his own subconscious in a manner anticipating the work of Freud and Jung.

SPIRITUAL DIARY
Swedenborg's private diary, which chronicles over twenty years of his visionary experiences.

THE ATHANASIAN CREED
A working MS exploring the relationship of Swedenborg's thought to early Christian doctrine.

CONJUGIAL LOVE
An extensive treatment of the implications of spiritual sexuality for marriage here on earth.

THE LAST JUDGMENT (Posthumous)
A working MS on the subtext of Christian apocalyptic expectations.

THE NEW JERUSALEM AND ITS HEAVENLY DOCTRINE
A concise survey of the distinctive terminology of *Arcana Coelestia*.

A VIEW FROM WITHIN
Compiled and translated by George F. Dole
A compendium of Swedenborg's theological thought in modern English.

See also:

THE UNIVERSAL HUMAN (A 1984 translation by Rev. George F. Dole, with preface by Dr. Stephen Larsen) New York, The Paulist Press, 1984. Excerpts from *Arcana Coelestia* on the symbolism of the human body; also includes Soul-Body Interaction (= Intercourse between the Soul and the Body), Swedenborg's most concise presentation of his cosmology.

Motion Pictures (Each available in 16mm, VHS, Beta, U-Matic, and other video formats)

SWEDENBORG: The Man Who Had to Know   30 minutes
Featuring Lillian Gish, narrated by Eddie Albert
Award-winning television docu-drama about Swedenborg's life and writings, with a script excerpted from his books, journals, and other eighteenth century accounts.

BLAKE: The Marriage of Heaven and Hell   30 minutes
Starring Anne Baxter and George Rose
Academy Award winner Anne Baxter and Tony Award winner George Rose re-create William Blake's inner world and artistic achievements, using Blake's own words, in this award-winning television docu-drama.

JOHNNY APPLESEED AND THE FRONTIER WITHIN   30 minutes
Starring veteran actor Joseph Davies and featuring Lillian Gish
This film explores the visionary side of John Chapman, 1774–1845, better known

as Johnny Appleseed. It shows another aspect of the man who was a friend of the Indian and settler alike, a planter of appleseeds as well as the spiritual seeds of Emanuel Swedenborg.

IMAGES OF KNOWING   15 minutes
A highly acclaimed, award-winning, lyrical exploration of the processes of nature as reflections of the processes of mind, written by Rev. George F. Dole.

THE OTHER SIDE OF LIFE   30 minutes
People who have had near-death experiences testify to a radically different view of themselves as a result. This lyrical film coordinates text and images to introduce the viewer to the deathless side of human nature—ideal for both counselors and individuals. Written by the Rev. George F. Dole. Narrated by Tony winner George Rose.

Send for Free Catalog:
Swedenborg Foundation, Inc.
139 East 23rd Street
New York, NY 10010

Bibliography

Keller, Helen. *My Religion.* New York: Swedenborg Foundation, 1953.

Moody, Dr. Raymond A., Jr. *Life After Life.* Atlanta: Mockingbird Books, 1975.

Odhner, Dr. Hugo Lj. *The Spiritual World.* Bryn Athyn, Pa.: Academy Publications Committee, 1968.

Sigstedt, Cyriel Odhner. *The Swedenborg Epic.* New York: Bookman, 1952.

Swedenborg, Emanuel. *Arcana Coelestia, The Heavenly Arcana.* Standard ed. New York: Swedenborg Foundation, 1967.

————. *The Apocalypse Explained.* Standard ed. New York: Swedenborg Foundation, 1968.

————. *Conjugial Love.* Standard ed. New York: Swedenborg Foundation, 1954.

————. *Heaven and Hell.* A modern translation by George F. Dole. New York: Swedenborg Foundation, 1976.

————. *The Spiritual Diary.* London: Swedenborg Society, 1962.

The Sacred Scripture (King James version). London: Swedenborg Society, 1949.